THE BASICS OF
LIBRARIANSHIP

THE BASICS OF LIBRARIANSHIP

Second edition

COLIN HARRISON
Head of School of Information Resources
Chelmer Institute of Higher Education

and

ROSEMARY BEENHAM
Senior Lecturer, School of Information Resources
Chelmer Institute of Higher Education

CLIVE BINGLEY LONDON

First published 1980 by Library Association Publishing Limited
Second impression with corrections 1981
This second, revised edition published 1985
Reprinted 1986
Reprinted 1987
Reprinted 1989

British Library Cataloguing in Publication Data

Harrison, Colin T.
    The basics of librarianship.—2nd ed.
    1. Library science
    I. Title   II. Beenham, Rosemary
    020   Z665

ISBN 0 85157 370 3

Contents

Authors' Note

Throughout this book we shall talk about library 'materials'. This form of shorthand is designed to save repeating a long list of items that modern libraries buy or make to enable them to provide their service. The list includes major items such as books, periodicals, records, tapes (sound and video), films, filmloops and strips, pictures, slides and computer services.

Libraries also provide equipment upon which the user can access the information contained in the various materials. Therefore, printer, record-player, slide viewer, cassette recorder, etc, will find their place in many libraries, in some to be lent out to the user, in others for use within the library only. All of these things, hardware and software, we put together as 'library materials'.

The book is designed for those taking the Technician/Business Education Council (B/TEC) Option Module Library and Information Work. It is also suitable for students who are taking the City and Guilds' Library Assistants Certificate and as a compact outline of librarianship for those going on to professional courses or for those studying for senior non-professional posts.

Chapter One

The functions of different types of library

The first question we need to answer in this chapter is exactly what we mean by 'function' and 'type' in the chapter title. Put simply, the function relates to what the library actually does for its users, while the type refers to a broad classification that links libraries having similar functions. In this book we have kept this broad classification down to a minimum number of types, namely, public libraries, academic libraries, industrial/commercial libraries and national libraries.

Some libraries may at first seem difficult to fit into this list of types: for example, a community library that is a branch of a public library but also serves as a school library. Obviously it could fit into the public or the academic classification. In fact, it goes into both and fulfils the functions of both, directing special services to the appropriate group of users. It is possible to list the functions it provides for the general public and those for the teachers and pupils — they will probably show some differences.

The broad function that lies at the heart of almost all library services is the provision of information and/or cultural materials. The proportion varies according to the aims and objectives of the particular service. For example, the public library service might be said to have a 40:60 split, while an industrial library will be wholly information-based.

The factors that decide this changing balance relate directly to the reasons for the existence of the service in the first place. Normally these reasons are embodied in a statement of policy or a series of aims and objectives that guide the day to day development and running of the service. We often find that 'industrial' libraries have more clearly defined terms of reference than public libraries. To some extent this reflects the environment in which the library operates, ie the economic world of industry where information is costed as part of the overall product price.

From this it follows that, whatever the type of library, it has a controlling body that monitors performance and development against the yardstick of the original objectives of the service. In almost no circumstances can the librarian be said to be the sole arbiter of what is or is not acceptable to the user. We are all answerable to a higher authority for the performance of ourselves, our staff and our service generally.

Mostly this control is vested in a committee representing those who provide the finance for the service. While librarians usually form part of the membership of the committee they seldom have enough influence to determine, singly, the outcome of any deliberations. Their strength rests in relating actions (proposed or taken) to original objectives and presenting a sound case to show how the two relate. In many libraries the cost-effectiveness of an action — for example, using computer services — is the most compelling argument for committee members.

What are these aims and objectives that form such an important part in the development of our services? Well, they vary greatly from place to place and from one type of library to another. Everyone working in a library ought to seek out and understand the precise aims and objectives of their particular library — usually the chief librarian will be able to produce them. There are, however, some generally agreed statements that can serve as introductory remarks to the aims and objectives of major types of libraries: public, national, academic, industrial, commercial, etc.

Public libraries

The aims of a public library can be said to be to contribute to the quality of life, to promote the concept of democratic society and to add to the sum total of man's happiness and awareness of himself, others and his environment.

To fulfil these aims particular objectives can be set that have been summarized as

1   *Education*
      To foster and provide means for the development of the individual/group at all levels of educational ability.

2 *Information*
   To give the user quick access to accurate information over the whole range of human knowledge.

3 *Culture*
   To be a chief centre for cultural life and to actively promote participation and appreciation of all the arts.

4 *Leisure and recreation*
   To play a positive part in encouraging an active use of leisure and recreational time.

The many services offered by our public libraries can be directly related to these aims and objectives, as can the selection of various materials and the organization of special events.

The history of the public library service dates back to before 1850, but that date marks the first Act of Parliament relating to libraries; others in 1919 and 1964 have assisted in developing the service and placing it firmly in the control of local authorities. In recent years this means, chiefly, putting it into the hands of county and metropolitan councils.

These authorities all have subcommittees of the council to advise them on policy relating to the development of the library service. Titles vary; many are called library subcommittees, in other places they may be combined into leisure or educational committees. Membership of the committee is usually in three parts:

   officers, eg librarian, architect, etc;
   elected members, that is local councillors;
   co-opted members, usually members of the public who have special knowledge of or interest in the subject of the committee, eg a local head teacher.

The officer members do not normally have voting rights, but, in conjunction with the chairman, prepare the agenda and any special reports for the consideration of members.

Items approved by the library committee often need to progress through other committees before reaching the full council — eg staffing matters may go to a personnel committee, finance to the finance committee — each of whom will comment on the suggestion being forwarded by the library committee.

Financial support for public libraries comes from the local rates (although these are to a large extent subsidized by central government via the rate support grant) and to this extent the will of the local community can determine the quality of the service. In most authorities you can obtain information showing how much of the rate, in percentage terms, is spent on libraries.

Because of this local raising of monies and the pressures that can be applied by residents on their councillor, the development of services could be influenced by pressure groups. It is to the credit of library committees and councils that this seldom happens and a more structured approach is employed.

Academic libraries
These range from the largest university libraries (some of which are virtually national libraries in that they obtain materials free of charge under the Copyright Acts) to the small school library. Each has a similar aim that may be expressed as 'to provide a service of reference and lending material appropriate to the needs of the staff and students of the instition'. These 'needs' can be very closely identified in the case of most academic libraries in that they reflect the courses offered and the research undertaken within the institution. In this respect an academic library may be less universal in its subject coverage than a public library.

General objectives may be listed as follows:
1   to serve the needs of the academic community (staff and students);
2   to provide reference materials at appropriate levels;
3   to provide study areas for users;
4   to provide a lending service appropriate to the different types of user;
5   to provide an active information service (and this may extend beyond the institution to local industry and commerce).

The extent to which each of these objectives is carried out depends upon the size and nature of the institution. Obviously a school library will not function in as developed a way as a polytechnic library — but its general aims will be similar.

Leaving aside the school library for the moment, a recognizably similar structure operates for other academic libraries, ie those of universities, polytechnics, institutions of higher education and further education colleges. Here the academic board (and it may have different titles in different institutions) represents the equivalent of the 'council'. It establishes the overall policy of the institution and monitors progress. Academic boards also set up subcommittees to deal with major areas of concern, one of which may be a library committee, or library matters may be dealt with as part of a larger group called resources or learning resources.

Senior members of the library staff are members of the committee as are other academics representing the 'users' of the service. The committee will operate much as the public library committee, referring matters to other committees, but ultimately to the academic board. Outside the university sector detailed discussions subsequently take place with the local education authority who provide the money for the institutions and are necessarily involved in plans requiring buildings and other large items needing financial support. The university would deal with the University Grants Committee on these matters.

School libraries differ significantly in that in many places they are provided as part of the county public library service and therefore control is not so directly vested in the school. However, many schools have 'councils' made up of staff and pupils who advise on the library and often select materials from visiting mobile libraries for inclusion in its stock. Larger schools may have a professional librarian, but too often this work is undertaken as an extra duty by teachers. Frequently in schools the collection is broken up into classrooms rather than contained in a central place. This is not unique to schools, however, since many universities, etc have subject department libraries as well as a main central library.

Industrial and commercial libraries
The chief aim of an industrial or commercial library can be expressed as 'to save the parent organization both time and money'. The general objectives can be summarized as follows:
1 the production and distribution of bulletins containing information relevant to the product, etc of the company;
2 the circulation of original materials to key staff according to their subject interest;
3 the provision of a collection designed to enable 1 and 2 above to be accomplished and to provide a base for research;

4   to provide staff to conduct literature searches on behalf of the research teams/management.

Many industrial libraries are finding that they need to use computer-based information systems to search literature and patent sources, so great is the reliance of these libraries on up to the minute information.

The place of the library within the organization is important if it is to be effective. Generally it is not associated with a particular department but is seen as part of the central provision, the librarian being responsible to the general manager, or a director, for the provision of the service.

Because of this direct relationship decisions are often easier to get in industrial libraries than in those previously discussed.

Because of the detailed knowledge required in this type of library, staffing may be of a different kind from that in other libraries. Often the professional staff of an industrial library will be a mix of professional scientists and librarians, and they are often called 'information officers' or 'scientists' rather than librarians.

Finance of the service will be seen as part of the total budget of the company and the librarian will have to submit estimates alongside other departments of the organization. It is at this stage that the cost of information is judged — is it cheaper to repeat research than to discover it has already been done and recorded? One well known commercial company says: 'The cost of finding information is high, the cost of not finding it is higher still.'

The libraries falling into this group range from those serving major manufacturers such as ICI or the Marconi Company, to small subscription libraries such as Lewis' Lending Library. In between there are a whole range of specialist services such as the specialist picture libraries used to supply photographs for books, television and publishing in general; record libraries such as the comprehensive one operated by the BBC to support its radio and television programmes. Almost all of the government and trade sponsored research associations also offer a library and information service to their members as do the major professional bodies such as The Library Association or trade unions. Many of these libraries also produce acquisitions lists which are circulated to members as part of their service.

National libraries

The focal point for a library service in the United Kingdom is the British Library. Through its major divisions it offers a comprehensive support service to libraries of all types throughout the United Kingdom. It is managed by the British Library Board which is responsible for the development of policy, this policy being implemented through the Executive of the British Library who are the heads of the five central divisions.

British Library
Board

| Lending Division | Bibliographic Division | Reference Division |

Administration   Research & Development

The Lending Division, which is based at Boston Spa in Yorkshire, was formed by the amalgamation of the National Central Library and the National Lending Library for Science and Technology. It now adds many thousands of items each year to its stock by the combination of purchase and international exchange. Its range of journals is one of the most comprehensive of any library in the world. Libraries may use the service through the medium of a prepaid voucher which covers the cost of handling and despatch or at the discretion of British Library photocopying or microfilming the document to be borrowed. In 1984 the cost of the voucher was £1.95.

The Reference Division is based on the old Department of Printed Books at the British Museum in London (one of the Copyright Deposit Libraries), the Department of Manuscripts and the Department of Oriental Manuscripts and Printed Books and the Science Reference Library. The Newspaper Library at Colindale is also part of the Reference Division. That part of the service which is still based in the British Museum is chiefly to be used as a library of last resort. By this we mean that users are expected to have exhausted the services and stocks of their local public and academic libraries before trying to gain access to that part of the Reference Division. Different criteria apply to using the Science Reference Library which because of its uniquely wide stock is a library of first as well as last resort. It is the country's premier research library for the natural sciences, engineering, technology and industrial property. The service is spread through seven buildings around London, three of which are open to the general public. These are the Southampton Buildings in Chancery Lane, often called the Holborn Reading Room, which specializes in United Kingdom patents, physical sciences and technologies and business information, Chancery House (also in Southampton Buildings) where on the lower ground floor there is a foreign patents reading room, and the Aldwych Reading Room in Kean Street which specializes in the life sciences and technologies, earth and space sciences and mathematics.

The Bibliographic Services Division is responsible for the production of the MARC (machine readable catalogue) which serves as the source for the production of the British National Bibliography and the MARC On-line Information Service which forms part of BLAISE. This division also cooperates in the production of the microfiche publication *Books in English*. The advent of new technology into libraries was exemplified through the introduction of the BLAISE On-line Information Services which have now spread to include such services as the British Education Index, audio/ visual information, and a whole host of medical bases accessed via America.

The research and development activities are of considerable importance in that they provide a national focus for the carrying out of research into a wide range of library and information related subjects. The Division provides funding for the setting up of work on approved projects and has an extensive publications activity to disseminate the results of research undertaken with its funds. Topics such as 'How to go on-line' and 'Library user education' are but two examples of research undertaken in recent years.

The whole of this service is designed as an umbrella to support the regional networks of library provision and therefore it is usual for local sources to be employed before application is made to the specialist national libraries. Much of the material added to the British library comes from its statutory right to receive free of charge one copy of everything published in the United Kingdom. The British Library zealously guards this right and uses agents to chase any material which it discovers being published but not supplied under the copyright deposit system.

Finance comes in two ways: the largest amount comes

from the Department of Education and Science in the form of grant-in-aid and the sum is approved annually in Parliament. The balance of the income is derived from the sale of services such as the British National Bibliography, on-line information services, research publications, inter-library loan vouchers, etc.

General finance
We have indicated how each type of library gets its income to provide its services. There is a common pattern of expenditure that can be dealt with fairly briefly.
The major items of expenditure are:

1 *Salaries*
Often half of total expenditure goes under this heading. It may also include training allowances, conference attendance, etc.

2 *Materials*
The second major item includes hardware and software. In public libraries books take the lion's share, but in academic and industrial libraries periodicals and similar current awareness sources take a large slice of this heading. Binding costs are also included in this area.

3 *Loan charges*
Repayments on the buildings and any repairs.

4 *Rates and rents*
Payable by all types of libraries.

5 *Energy bill*
Heating, lighting, etc.

6 *General*
In some libraries printing, furniture, equipment, etc are separate heads of expenditure and may appear so on budgets.

The balance between these items will vary from library to library but most libraries can show a budget or allocation that conforms to the general pattern given above.

Project work
1 Produce a diagram showing how your library relates to its parent organization. In particular show how it relates to any committee structure that exists.

2   List the major headings of expenditure in your library and show the proportion of the global budget each takes.

3   Write a brief statement giving the aims and objectives of your library. Discuss this with a senior member of the library to see if your perceptions actually fit the real objectives. You might find it useful to go into some detail if major differences are revealed.

4   Classify your library as one of the major types given in Chapter One. Compare and contrast the details given in the book with what your library actually does. Can you discover reasons for any differences?

5   Suggest ways in which your library could develop/improve its services better to meet its aims and objectives. Do a simple costing of these developments and relate this to a head of budget expenditure.

Chapter Two

Organization, management and training of staff

The effectiveness of any library service depends to a large extent upon the manner in which the staff and their duties are organized. Few librarians ever have the opportunity of starting a brand new service in new buildings with new staff, so most of them are faced with the continual modification of an existing structure. 'Existing structure' is an impersonal way of saying we are dealing with people — members of staff — who have a perception of their role and place in the structure and will often feel under threat when changes are being considered. The sensitive manager, therefore, will take great trouble to discuss changes with his staff and keep them fully informed about how they personally will be affected should the changes ultimately be approved. In conducting these changes the manager will soon become aware that in most organizations there are two types of structure operating simultaneously. There is the formal structure, as represented by an organization chart, that forms the basis of the hierarchy and interrelationships of the system, and the informal structure which represents how people actually relate one to another. It is seldom that the two correlate very closely. It can happen, therefore, that changes on the formal organization chart that appear not to affect an individual may in fact affect him or her in an important way because they can be thought to damage his or her informal relationships.

Organization charts
Formal structures are represented in a hierarchical fashion on an organization chart and are defined more closely in individual job descriptions. Typical examples of organization charts are given in Figures 1 and 2. The first represents the

SENIOR MANAGEMENT TEAM

COUNTY LIBRARIAN
DEPUTY COUNTY LIBRARIAN

Principal Asst. Librarian
LEISURE

Recreational use of libraries
Cultural activities
Co-ordination with cultural/
  Leisure organizations
Display and publicity
Professional staff training

Principal Asst. Librarian
YOUNG PEOPLE & EDUCATION

Schools
Colleges
University
Pre-school playgroups
Other educational institutions
Public library education
  co-ordination

Principal Asst. Librarian
ADMINISTRATION

Estimates/Expenditure
Transport
Staff administration
Stationery stores
Accounts
Buildings

Principal Asst. Librarian
BIBLIOGRAPHICAL SERVICE

Interlending
Stock co-ordination
Stock administration
Stock supply
Classification
Cataloguing
Management of Central
  resource area
Subject departments

Principal Asst. Librarian
SPECIAL SERVICES

Information services
Hospitals
Handicapped
Disadvantaged
Museums
Prisons

North & West Essex
Divisional Libraries

Staff control training
Staff appointments
Stock control
Readers' service
Public relations liaison
Services to education
Services to the
  disadvantages
Service to individuals

Buckhurst Hill	Ongar
Chigwell	Potter St
Debden	Roydon
Epping	Saffron
Gt Parndon	Walden
Harlow	Standsted
Loughton	Thaxted
Market Hill	Theydon
Nazeing	Bois
Nth Weald	Tye Green
Old Harlow	Waltham
	Abbey
	3 Mobiles

South West Essex
Divisional Librarian

Staff control training
Staff appointments
Stock control
Readers' service
Public relations liaison
Services to education
Services to the
  disadvantages
Service to individuals

Aveley	Fryerns
Basildon	Grays
Belhus	Hutton
Billericay	Ingatestone
Bishops Hall	Laindon
Blackmore	Shenfield
Blackshotts	Stanford le
Brentwood	Hope
Chadwell St	Tilbury
Mary	Vange
Corrington	West
East Tilbury	Horndon
	2 Mobiles

South East Essex
Divisional Librarian

Staff control training
Staff appointments
Stock control
Readers' service
Public relations liaison
Services to education
Services to the
  disadvantages
Service to individuals

Ashington	Rayleigh
Canvey	Rochford
Friars	S. Benfleet
Gt Tarpots	Southchurch
Gt Wakering	Southend
Hadleigh	Temple
Hawkwell	Sutton
Hockley	Thorpe-
Hullbridge	dene
Kent Elms	Westcliff
Leigh	Wickford
	2 Mobiles

Central Essex
Divisional Librarian

Staff control training
Staff appointments
Stock control
Readers' service
Public relations liaison
Services to education
Services to the
  disadvantaged
Service to individuals

Bicknacre	Hay Lane
Bocking	Heybridge
Braintree	Maldon
Broomfield	Silver End
Burnham	S'thminster
Chelmsford	Sth Woodham
Coggeshall	Ferrers
Danbury	Stock
Dunmow	Wickham
Galleywood	Bishops
Gt Baddow	Witham
Hatfield	Writtle
Peverel	4 Mobiles

North East Essex
Divisional Librarian

Staff control training
Staff appointments
Stock control
Readers' service
Public relations liaison
Services to education
Services to the
  disadvantaged
Service to individuals

Brighlingsea	Parkeston
Clacton	Prettygate
Colchester	Rowhedge
Earls Colne	Sible
Frinton	Hedingham
Greenstead	Stanway
Halstead	Tiptree
Harwich	Walton
Holland	West
Jaywick	Mersea
Kelvedon	Wivenhoe
Manaingtree	3 Mobiles

Figure 1: 1984 structure of Essex County Library Service

structure of one of the largest county library services in the country while the second represents a typical medium-sized academic library. The charts can show the number of staff and the salary grades of the posts and the relationships between the different levels of management and employees. The production of one of these formal charts is a prerequisite to an understanding of the operation of a system. Many commercial organizations conduct searches among their employees to discover to whom those employees actually report in practice and with whom they have written or verbal communication as a regular part of their duties. By comparing this informal communication network with the formal organization chart one can see how close the fit between actuality and theory is. Provided that key people are not being circumvented by the informal structure a certain looseness of fit is quite acceptable.

The next stage in this process of looking at the structure of the organization is to define the actual duties allocated to each individual and to ensure that as far as is practical the group of duties allocated to each person is a fair quantity of work for him to perform.

Job description

What is a job description? It is a detailed list of duties expected of a particular post and it shows to whom the post holder is directly responsible. Often the job description is combined with a personnel specification. This is an attempt to describe the sort of person who could adequately perform the duties given in the job description. The factors that one would take into account in producing a personnel specification would be:

1 *Physical ability*
   That is to say, does the job require long periods of standing?

2 *Age*
   Is there any reason to limit people applying for the post to a particular age range?

3 *Qualifications*
   What qualifications do you actually need in order to perform the duties? Could you justify asking for a specific qualification for the work given in the job description?

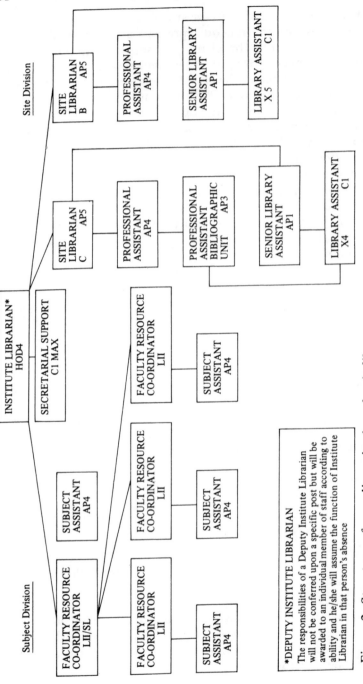

Figure 2: Structure of a medium-sized academic library

These are the sorts of questions that one would wish to consider when drawing up a personnel specification.

It is clear that the job description and the personnel specification are closely related and they are often produced as a single document which is sent to applicants to help them to assess their suitability for the post.

GENERAL LIBRARY ASSISTANT

Non-professional staff may be required to undertake any of the following activities. In general, however, some activities are allocated specifically to a particular member of staff.

1 *Issuing and renewals* Charging all material borrowed by members of the public. Amending loan records and recording renewals.

2 *Discharging material* Discharging material on loan.

3 *Issue maintenance* Moving up, filing and counting issue.

4 *Cancellation of issue* Cancellation of any written issue record.

5 *Sorting returned material* All sorting of material between return and shelving, e.g. for repairs and shelving.

6 *Shelving* Taking returned material to shelves and filing away. Moving stock to enable shelving to take place.

7 *Shelf tidying* Putting material in order on shelves and straightening.

8 *Maintaining readers' records* Registration and re-registration of borrowers. Making out tickets. Maintenance of membership records.

9 *Overdues* Preparation of issue records prior to overdue writing. Extraction of data from issue records. Writing overdues including accounts, instructions to book recovery officers, overdues to other libraries. Checking shelves and stock records before writing or despatch of overdues. Monitoring computer printouts as necessary.

10 *Reservations* Receipt of handling of reservations. Catalogue, shelf and issue checking. Routine bibliographical checking. Listing of reservations. Checking returned material against lists. All inter-library loan procedures including requesting material by telex, checking circulated reservation lists, etc.

11 *Ordering stock* Pre-ordering routines, e.g. checking bibliographical details, stock holdings, etc. Clerical aspects of ordering and follow-up procedures.

12 *Processing stock* Preparing material for addition to stock. Sorting stock records preparatory to filing. Inserting security triggers.

13 *Periodicals* Recording receipt. Display and filing. Maintaining records of holdings. Preparation for binding. Circulation procedures.

14 *Stock editing* Clerical procedures connected with stock editing.

15 *Repairs* Physical upkeep including cleaning, replacement of issue stationery and class marks, general repairs, insertion of triggers.

16 *Re-binding* Clerical procedures connected with binding, e.g. compiling records of material sent to binding; packing and unpacking; checking returned material and completion of processing. Amendment of stock records.

17 *Typing and duplicating* of handouts and catalogue records and correspondence.

18 *Film ordering service.*

19 *Withdrawals* Removal and amendment of stock records. Offering selected material to other locations. Disposal of withdrawn material.

20 *Stocktaking* Comparison of stock records with stock and issue.

21 *Inquiries* Directional inquiries and other routine inquiries which can properly be resolved by non-professional staff.

22 *Telephone.*

23 *Displays and extension activities* Putting up notices. Preparation and mounting of displays. Assisting with story hours and class visits.

24 *General administration* Statistics, accounts and cash handling, timetables, mail. General administration of service point.

25 *Information file maintenance* Updating information files.

26 *Filing pamphlet material,* e.g. standards, printed catalogues, prospectuses.

27 *Photocopying* Includes making photocopies, dealing with declaration forms and payments. Control of photocopier and similar machinery. Sales of tokens to operate machines.

28 *Amendments* Transferring information received from amending services to appropriate publications. Updating reference material from current sources.

29 *Office Supplies*

30 *Security system* Operation of system, including checking bags, etc. as necessary.

31 *Education training* Attendance at in-service training courses and general education as appropriate to the post.

32 Duties of the post may be varied, and or changed, from time to time as required.

Figure 3: Example of a job description

In many cases, because of the similar nature of the duties, a job description is prepared for a particular group of posts, eg senior library assistants or general library assistants. Depending upon the size and nature of the library service, the personnel specification may vary for people applying for posts within the same group. An example of a job description for a general library assistant is given in Figure 3. You will notice that some 32 tasks are identified as being appropriate to this post. In a small library the one or two members of staff falling into this group might well need to be trained in all of these. In a large county library service there may well be sufficient work in any grouping of two or three to keep staff fully occupied. Therefore, in drawing up the personnel description the abilities and qualifications that one is seeking will be directly related to the particular duties being advertised at that time. A practical example of this could be the grouping together of the following areas of work: 17, 18, 22, 25 and 29. For this group of tasks one would be seeking an applicant who had office/clerical qualifications, who had a pleasant voice for the telephone and perhaps a proven record of competence in the filing and handling of materials. However, if you take tasks 5, 6 and 7 you would be looking for somebody who is physically fit, who is numerate and literate and perhaps has a high boredom threshold.

An example of a combined job and personnel description for a more senior post in an academic library is given in Figure 4.

Work studies
Now we can turn to the day to day monitoring of how the work system operates. No organization can remain static, and as changes occur these will affect, sometimes dramatically, the loading on each individual task. A regular review of what is involved in each task must be undertaken to ensure a continued fair distribution of work. It is often considered to be the role of the senior library assistant to monitor this on a day to day basis and report any inequalities to a superior as soon as changes are needed. Routine supervision of people working is the usual way of monitoring problems. In some libraries this is supported by the application of simple work study techniques devised both to monitor work rates and to enable workers to suggest improvements in routines. By

---

JOB DESCRIPTION
A FACULTY RESOURCES CO-ORDINATOR

The person occupying this post will be responsible directly to the Institute Librarian for the performance of the following duties:

1 To know the detailed structure and educational goals of the courses in the Faculty, including the way they are administered, the methods of teaching and learning employed on the courses, and the relevant characteristics and problems of their students. To know the courses' entry requirements, validation process and assessment methods.

2 To obtain after appointment such subject knowledge of the topics covered by the courses as to make possible an understanding of the syllabus's content, range and emphasis and in particular to obtain detailed knowledge of [to be specified] courses.

3 To obtain after appointment some understanding of current developments in educational thought and practice.

4 To possess a high degree of competence in professional academic librarianship.

5 To have some familiarity with non-print material and with media equipment, and to gain after appointment some experience of media production.

6 To serve on the relevant course boards, committees and working parties in order to:
   (a) understand the courses' resource needs and to evaluate these in qualitative, quantitative and financial terms;
   (b) draw attention to the range of resources and facilities provided by the Institute's Library resources;
   (c) support and encourage within the courses the development of new approaches to teaching and learning;
   (d) convey information about course developments and needs to both academic staff and the appropriate Library staff.

7 In the study of [to be specified] to be aware of all significant works and sources of information for the courses, so as to be able to select and provide bibliographic records of stock, and to develop the collection to its maximum level of effectiveness; and to ensure that the collection contains all relevant formats of material, both print and non-print.

8 To apply the techniques of a professional librarian to ensure that resources are exploited fully, such exploitation to include:
   (a) the selective dissemination of information;
   (b) the critical analysis of library materials for information retrieval purposes;
   (c) the introduction of staff and students to the range and depth of resources available both within the Institute and elsewhere; formal and information instruction in the use of Library resources;
   (d) to provide an information desk service within the Libraries.

9 To provide academic leadership under the overall direction of the Institute Librarian to those members of the Library staff offering specific services into the Faculty of [to be specified]. To advise the Institute Librarian on the general developments and in particular needs of the courses within the Faculty so that adequate financial provision can be made for further growth and to ensure that the Library service develops its provision in accordance with the needs of staff and students within that Faculty.

Figure 4: Combined job and personnel description

observing the work rate of reliable assistants or even by asking them to keep a record of how long certain tasks take, it is possible to calculate an average time to perform these duties. This information can be used to monitor workloads. It is important to explain to the staff exactly what you are doing and why you are doing it, and to make it clear that if they have any doubts or concerns regarding the practice they should consult their workplace representative or union official. Major work study is best left to the professionals and these are usually available within each county, metropolitan or business organization. A major national report, LAMSAC,[1] concerned itself with the study of the staffing of public libraries. This lengthy document is of considerable use to librarians in all sorts of libraries and is worthy of study.

Some of the various factors of which you will wish to take

account in any assessment of staffing levels following an organization and methods (O & M) survey are as follows:

1 The number of hours the library is open and the number of people required on duty for each hour.
2 The number of separate service points to be manned.
3 Inquiry desks — level of manning required at each part of the day.
4 Volume of processing work to be accomplished.
5 Book ordering and invoice checking, etc — number of staff necessary to ensure that delays do not occur.
6 Cataloguing and classification.
7 Professional support services in terms of book lists, reading lists, etc.
8 Staff training time — it is normal to make an allowance so that staff can be trained internally and can be released for education on outside courses.
9 Sickness cover — in many libraries there is a central pool of staff to offer sickness relief to branches and central departments.
10 Extension activities — these often make great demands on staff, particularly in public libraries where personnel may be involved in the organization of exhibitions or series of lectures.
11 Committees, working parties, staff development duties —although this work will normally be undertaken by senior staff as part of their duties, where there are a large number of internal working parties the time used in attending these should be taken into account.

Interviewing

The object of the interview is to enable the two parties to assess each other so that when an appointment is made an employer selects as an employee a candidate who actually wants to do the job. To achieve this desirable end, the method of interview has to be structured to overcome the totally artificial atmosphere that can so easily be induced. This is not to say that the formal interview across a table has no place in selection procedures since the stress it normally occasions is often replicated in real life when things go wrong. Requiring the interviewee to operate under some degree of pressure is in reality a fair test of his ability. The following methods can be employed to give candidates a more balanced interview and also to involve more of the library staff in the procedure:

1   *Tour of workplace*
    The object of this is to enable candidates to look at the physical surroundings in which they would be working and to give them a chance to talk informally with members of staff performing functions similar to those covered by the job for which they are applying. It is helpful to involve senior library assistants, etc who can talk with candidates informally, either in a group or individually, and who will often form useful impressions of their suitability. These views should be passed to any later interviewing panel to form part of the overall assessment of an applicant's suitability for the post.

2   *Testing*
    In too few cases do librarians seek any practical evidence that applicants are capable of performing the jobs for which they are applying. It is neither unfair nor unreasonable to expect candidates to be willing to undertake a limited range of practical tests such as putting a shelf of books in order, typing a page of text, perhaps putting plastic jackets on books, etc. This is also helpful for the candidate since it gives him, perhaps for the first time, a chance to appreciate what he will be spending many hours doing in future.

3   *Formal interviews*
    The formal interview in which the candidate is faced by a panel often composed of the librarian, the personnel officer and a few other individuals is traditional. All too often the size of the interviewing panel is out of all proportion to the salary being offered for the job advertised, and while it may be appropriate to have half a dozen people interviewing for a senior professional post, two or three are more than adequate for more junior posts.
    In conducting these interviews the chairman should always allow a settling-in period so that the candidate can answer relatively simple, general questions before the session focuses on the more germane assessments. In formulating questions to ask the candidate the interviewers have three basic tools to assist them: they have

the applicant's own application form, the job description and the personnel description. By seeing how closely the applicant's history, qualifications, age, etc match up to the personnel description, areas that need to be explored normally become evident.

The technique of questioning at these interviews is that you start with the general or 'open-ended' question to get the candidate talking. An example of this might be: 'What particular jobs do you enjoy most in your present post?' Once the candidate has answered this general question you might well follow it up with a question probing the areas that he did not like, such as: 'What in particular did you not enjoy about shelving books?' In this way your first general question does not give away too much of your own attitudes or expectations and therefore the candidate will find it easier to answer the questions truthfully than to provide an answer that he thinks you expect. Towards the end of the time available for the interview one should always allow a period when the candidate can ask questions of the panel. Often these questions will be related to salaries, conditions of service starting dates, etc, but will occasionally produce more interesting questions, and these may well give an insight into the character of the applicant.

The expert interviewer will make notes on his feelings about each applicant relating to individual areas of questioning so that by the end of a morning's interviewing he has sufficient notes to allow a fair assessment of the candidates who appeared early on the list.

4   *Group interviews*
While this technique would normally only be used for higher professional posts, it is occasionally used for posts at all levels. Here the candidates are brought together and given the opportunity of joining in a general discussion with members of the interviewing panel. Often this is extended over a luncheon period so that the social skills of the candidates can also be measured. This can be an extremely helpful technique when used in the appropriate circumstances.

Professional and non-professional duties

With the spread of O & M studies into the library world over the last 20 years it has become increasingly the case that the work of people in libraries has been categorized into professional and non-professional duties. While there were always professional and non-professional staff in libraries it was often difficult, particularly in small libraries, to distinguish clearly the boundary between the two areas. This was simply because there was often only one member of staff on duty and he performed all of the jobs without concern for demarcation. In the modern world, since professional status and salary levels are often determined by the way the post is created, in O and M studies it has become increasingly important to identify tasks which are the chief prerogative of the professionally qualified librarian and those which can be performed by suitably trained library assistants. Referring back to Figure 3, you will see that all of the tasks on this list are of a non-professional nature. When preparing job descriptions it is important to take account of the nature of the duties to ensure that you are not asking professional staff to perform too wide a range of non-professional duties and, perhaps more importantly, vice versa. The Library Association publishes a comprehensive list[2] of professional and non-professional duties and this should be read in some detail to ensure a proper understanding of the boundaries between the two areas of responsibility. In its introduction this publication says:

> It is this characteristic, the possession of an intellectual technique acquired by special training which can be applied to some sphere of everyday life, that forms the distinguishing mark of a profession. Applying these definitions to librarianship, it may be said that 'professional' duties are those whose adequate performance involves the ability to exercise independent judgement based on an understanding of the principles of library service — publications and information users and the means by which they are brought into effective relationship.

Table 1 is an outline of the major areas covered by this publication.

Normally a degree in librarianship or its equivalent is required for professional posts while non-professional posts will be filled by staff having success at 'O' and 'A' levels,

Table 1 PROFESSIONAL AND NON-PROFESSIONAL DUTIES IN LIBRARIES		
Area of work	Professional	Non-professional

1 ADMINISTRATION	OBJECTIVES
	POLICY to implement objectives
	PLANNING — long-term
	           — short-term
	
	BUDGET
	SUPERVISION of staff
	RULES and REGULATIONS
	REPORT WRITING
		BOOKKEEPING
		Routine orders
		Petty cash — receipt
		Petty cash — disbursement
		Maintenance of records
		MAIL
		   In-coming
		   Out-going
		   Filing
		OFFICE ROUTINES
		   Taking minutes
		   Typing
		   Duplicating
		   Telephone
		   Telex
		   Reception
		STOCK
		   Receipt
		   Inventories

2 PERSONNEL MANAGEMENT	JOB EVALUATION STAFF ESTABLISHMENT RECRUITMENT IN-SERVICE TRAINING STAFF WELFARE	TRAINING of junior non-professionals

Area of work	Professional	Non-professional
3 PUBLIC RELATIONS	PUBLICITY CONTACT WITH COMMUNITY EXTRA-LIBRARY ACTIVITIES, e.g. talks, film shows, visits	Publicity records, e.g. scrap-book Preparation of publicity material Distribution of publicity material Mailing lists
4 STOCK SELECTION	POLICIES ALLOCATING FUNDS SCANNING REVIEWS, etc. CONTROL OF BUDGET	CHECKING CATALOGUE PREPARING ORDERS CHASING ORDERS CORRESPONDENCE with suppliers KEEPING BUDGET RECORDS RECEIPT & PROCESSING
5 STOCK EDITING	CONTINUOUS CONTROL (Demand/supply)	Assistance in stock editing
6 STOCK WITHDRAWALS	POLICIES	Preparing lists of material available for offer Withdrawing catalogue entries

Area of work	Professional	Non-professional
7 CATALOGUING	POLICIES e.g. Type of catalogue Form of catalogue Full/simplified cataloguing Total/selective cataloguing Cataloguing rules, etc. DESCRIPTIVE CATALOGUING ADDED ENTRIES, etc. CHECKING THE FILING OF ENTRIES GUIDING AUTHORITY FILE	Producing catalogue entries from a master Simplified cataloguing Filing catalogue entries
8 CLASSIFICATION	POLICIES e.g. Choice of scheme Broken order, etc. CLASSIFICATION	Lettering spines Adding class number to issue stationery
9 STOCK MAINTENANCE i.e. binding, repair	POLICIES DECISIONS CHECKING PROCESSES	Jacketing Repairs, reinforcing Preparation for binding Dispatch to bindery Receipt from bindery Binding expenditure records Tidying shelves

Area of work	Professional	Non-professional
10 STOCK CONTROL & SECURITY	STOCKTAKING POLICY STOCKTAKING SUPERVISION SECURITY ARRANGEMENTS	Applying ownership labels Stocktaking
11 ASSISTANCE TO READERS	POLICIES e.g. Scope 　　Organization INSTRUCTION TO READERS 　(a) individuals 　(b) groups ANSWERING INQUIRIES READING GUIDANCE CIRCULATION OF INFORMATION ABSTRACTING COMPILATION OF BIBLIOGRAPHIES	SIMPLE INQUIRIES Checking catalogue Checking bibliographies
12 LOANS	POLICIES e.g. Rules and regulations 　　Charging system 　　Membership stationery 　　Inter-library loans ANALYSIS OF ISSUE STATISTICS HANDLING COMPLAINTS	Registering borrowers Explaining rules Charging Discharging Renewals Reservations Overdues Fines Issue statistics Membership statistics

City and Guilds Library Assistants Certificate or the Technician/BEC Business Education Council examination with the special library studies module. This latter examination will probably be considered the appropriate grade for promotion to posts of senior library assistant in public and other libraries.

Induction and training
An essential requirement for all non-professional posts (and many professional posts) is appropriate induction into the service where new staff meet colleagues and see how each department relates to the others. The induction course will give all the necessary employment details and conditions of service relating to such matters as the amount of leave entitlement, an explanation of the contract of employment, insurance stoppages, what to do in case of sickness and how to inform senior colleagues when not being able to attend for duty, etc. Equally important, it will provide a background to the social structure of the library — the staff guild, any clubs or unions that operate within the library, discount schemes, car parking facilities, arrangements for meals, etc.

This early opportunity should also be taken to impress upon the new entrant the right attitudes to work and to the public. Much of this information is best reinforced by the production of a staff notebook that can be given to every new entrant. The notebook should also contain a list of the staff and an explanation of the departmental structures so that relationships can be learned easily and the right people contacted from the outset. The induction procedure must occur immediately after joining, otherwise bad habits will be formed and will be difficult to eradicate.

Training is a more structured and long-term project. Initial training will probably take place in the individual department or library where the new entrant works, and he or she will be guided and instructed by responsible assistants so that he gradually learns the background to the total service. It is often helpful to formalize this training procedure by the use of some simple form that enables the new assistant to check which tasks he has been trained to do and by whom he has been trained, and it should also allow either party to make comments about the training given. A simple example of this is given in Figure 5. In this case the duty numbers relate to the duties listed in Figure 3. The new assistant should be allowed to keep a copy for his own personal use while the carbon copy can be kept in his personal file as a permanent record of his training. This basic in-service training should always be supplemented by a staff manual of practice to which any member of staff can refer to refresh his memory about particular methods of operation or the library's basic policy decisions.

Once the initial in-service training has been completed,

TRAINING SCHEDULE

DUTY	INSTRUCTED BY	DATE	COMMENTS	SIGNED AS HAVING RECEIVED INSTRUCTION
1				
2				
3				
4				
5				
6				
7				
8				
9				
10				
11				
12				
13				

Figure 5 Training schedule

more extended training may well be considered advisable. In large library systems this may involve attendance on short courses run by the library training officer. In some cases it could mean attendance on courses at colleges in the area or it might take the form of attendance at meetings of local groups of librarians. Membership of The Library Association brings staff into contact with people in their region and employed in their particular type of library service. These meetings are valuable since they allow an exchange of views and techniques between colleagues at all levels.

Extended training is perhaps better described as a mixture of training and education, since the term 'training' is normally applied to more practical skills acquisition rather than the broader philosophical problems to which the courses we have just been talking about would lead. Finance for these training/ education courses can often be obtained from the local education authority, particularly where attendance on recognized courses is involved, or from the local government training board or one of the other industrial training boards. Many employers will also allow staff to be given time off work to attend courses over and above their normal holiday entitlement.

The object of this training is to enable the assistant to perform his duties satisfactorily, to enable him to see how his work fits into the total service, to give him job satisfaction and, finally, to widen his education in library matters so that he begins to appreciate the role of the service regionally and nationally.

In most authorities the new entrant will be employed for a probationary period. The length of probation may well vary, but the reason for it is to enable the employer and the employee to assess one another. Obviously if the employee is dissatisfied with the job he will look for another post. If the employer is dissatisfied with the way the assistant is responding to training he may well wish to consider invoking the probation clause in the letter of appointment. If this is to be done, it is important that adequate warnings be given to the employee throughout the period of probation. These should include written warnings indicating very clearly the areas where dissatisfaction is being occasioned. It is equally important that additional training is given to allow the assistant further opportunity to improve his performance. Copies of all correspondence must be included in the individual's personal file. Attention is drawn to the Contracts of Employment Act of 1972 and to the National Joint Council's *Scheme of conditions of service* (the purple book) and other nationally agreed schemes relating to the conditions of employment in particular areas.

Supervisory duties
The supervisor needs at least a little understanding of motivation and behaviour. Reference should be made to Chapter Ten of *Management techniques for librarians*.[3] Perhaps we could summarize the problem as a recognition that every employee has 'needs'. These will vary, not only from person to person, but from time to time with each person. According to A H Maslow's *Theory of human motivation* there are five levels of need, which are:

1   Physical needs — these are often associated with bodily comfort. It is therefore important for the supervisor to take account of room temperatures, both hot and cold; the freshness of the air and the adequacy of ventilation; levels of lighting; decoration; canteen facilities, etc.
2   Security needs — a basic need of most people since this applies to security both regarding employment and home life. From the supervisor's point of view it is worth bearing in mind that to exercise disciplinary control through threats may well be self-defeating since these threats will attack this basic need.
3   Social needs — this covers such things as acceptance by fellow workers and integration into the informal structures of the organization.
4   Esteem needs — this covers not only how the individual sees his own role but also his perception of how others see him. This need can be influenced by only offering criticism in private but by giving praise in public.
5   Self-actualization or the need to realize one's potential — training, education and promotion all play their parts in this need.

A basic understanding of what motivates each individual helps a supervisor plan the right approach. Generally it is sound to assume competence, to involve people in decision making, to take opinions into account — this helps create an atmosphere of trust, harmony and co-operation. Where problems do arise it is sensible to check out the training programme before blaming the assistant for poor performance of duties. However, after full investigation, if the assistant has been trained properly, is capable of performing the duties accurately but is just not performing them satisfactorily, it is essential that the supervisor takes the assistant aside and attempts to discover the reason for the problems and try to overcome them. It could sometimes be of help to use the services of welfare or personnel officers since often people will talk to outsiders rather more easily than they can talk to their immediate superiors.

Supervisors do have an important responsibility to the organization, and if in spite of all this care and attention there are still staff who are causing problems because (1) they were selected for the wrong job, (2) they feel some sense of grievance and are therefore being obstructive, or (3) they are just not able to handle certain tasks, the supervisor has a clear responsibility to give adequate warnings as to future conduct, to ensure complete training is given, to follow this up with written warnings and, if necessary, make contact with union representatives.

Personal records
From all of the foregoing the need to keep clear, confidential records will be apparent. Accuracy of information is vital and particular care must be taken to record joining dates, changes of post, salary levels, etc, quickly and correctly. Only appropriate staff will be allowed access to these files, since they contain very sensitive information. Staff who do have access must be selected for their discretion and must never use their knowledge except in the performance of their duties.

In many libraries, these records will be in two forms. The first is a simple card which contains the 'core' details of each employee; an example is given in Figure 6. This is supported by an individual file which contains copies of all documents regarding the individual from the time he first applied for the post. The file will start with the job description and personnel description, and will contain copies of the advertisement, the completed application form, references taken up, comments made during interview and the letter of appointment. Once the new member is in post, letters relating to changes in conditions of employment and letters of commendation or

		Department
		. . . .

SURNAME . . . .   Christian names . . . .

Single name . . . .   Date of Birth . . . .
(If married woman)

Post . . . . Grading . . . .   Private Address . . . .

Qualifications . . . .

Date of   Superann.   . . . .
Appointment . . . .   IN/OUT   Telephone no. . . . .

Date of resignation . . . .

National Insurance Number   /   /   /   /   Vice-

Date	Salary	Reason for Change	Courses attended and results	Remarks

Figure 6 Employee's record card

warnings as to future conduct, etc would be placed in the file.
The file would obviously conclude with the letter of resignation.

After resignation the file is usually kept in store for several
years after which time it may well be microcopied and the
original destroyed. The reason for keeping the file in its
original state for a few years after the member of staff has
left is that quite often he will give his old employer's name as
a reference. Copies of any references given should be added
to the file.

Increasingly this manual system of keeping records is
being replaced by computerized systems, in some cases
linked to a microfilm store; in other cases edge-punched card
systems are used. Obviously this use of automation extends
the usefulness of the staff records since by careful encoding
of information personnel officers can achieve useful statistical comparisons, eg all the staff who have a certain qualification.

Welfare
This can be considered in two parts, statutory and social.

1   *Statutory*
      There are Acts of Parliament that lay down basic con-
      ditions of work and safety regulations that affect every

employee. The Offices, Shops and Railway Premises Act, 1963, and the Health and Safety at Work Act, 1974, are the major pieces of legislation that must be considered. These Acts make it clear that certain basic requirements must be met before staff can be expected to work. Such things as the minimum room temperature within one hour of starting work, the adequacy of light and ventilation, toilet provision, fire regulations and exits and the safety of electrical appliances are all covered in considerable detail.

While every member of staff has a duty under the Acts to be observant where safety is concerned, it is inevitable that the chief responsibility must rest with the various levels of management. Staff showing signs of illness or injury should be sent to the medical centre and any necessary accident or safety forms completed. It is essential that once completed these forms are acted upon and not just filed away. In cases where compliance with the Acts is in doubt professional help can often be obtained from safety officers or inspectors who can be contacted through the local councils.

2   *Social*
Many large libraries have staff associations. These provide a mixture of entertainment, discount trading arrangements with local firms and a forum to discuss matters relating to working conditions or the development of the service. In some library authorities these associations are highly developed and form a positive bridge between junior staff and the senior management.

All libraries will have a majority of their staff who belong to trade unions. To some extent local authorities take a corporate attitude to how freely they allow the operation of the union or its representatives within their departments, and this general attitude will cover the library. Generally staff are allowed to attend meetings provided the service is not disrupted, and in some places staff are allowed time off their normal duties to act as workplace representatives or to hold other official positions representing the union interests of workers. In terms of management, it is helpful to keep the appropriate union representative informed of changes of policy, etc that affect his members. The staff association should also be kept informed so that non-union members are not discriminated against. This course of action can lead to both unions and staff associations providing positive help in the implementation of changes.

In larger library systems there will be a welfare or personnel officer who can assist staff with personal problems relating to home life or their employment. The sympathetic supervisor will be on the lookout for signs that staff require this type of assistance and will act in a positive way to encourage staff to make use of all the counselling facilities that may be available to them, not only within the library service but also within the council or firm as a whole.

References

1 Department of Education and Science. *The staffing of public libraries.* 3 vols. London, HMSO, 1976.
2 Library Association. *Professional and non-professional duties in libraries.* London, Library Association, 1974. (Now out of print and partially replaced by 'Duties and responsibilities of library staffs', Library Association *Record*, 86: 307-9, 1984.)
3 Evans, G E *Management techniques for librarians.* Academic Press, 1976. 163-86.

Bibliography

Corbett, E V *Fundamentals of library organization and administration.* London, Library Association, 1978. 137-70.

Edwards, R J *In-service training in British libraries.* London, Library Association, 1976.

Harrison, C T *Communication in library management.* AAL/SED, 1979.

Project work

1 Produce an organization chart for the library in which you work. Visit another, different type of library and see if you can produce an organization chart for it.
2 Using the charts from (1) above, look for differences in the structure, and account for them in terms of aims and objectives and job functions.

3   Design a staff record card and show the need for the information it would contain.
4   Describe the relationship between the staff in your library and their union(s).
5   Show how communications flow up and down the 'tree' in your library.
6   Devise an in-service training course for a new, junior member of staff.

Chapter Three

Acquisition of basic library materials

The modern library service calls upon a wide range of materials with which to provide its service to users. The acquisition of these materials is a skilful job demanding the sort of dedication that a housewife brings to the running of her home. In spite of the fact that books are controlled as far as their price is concerned and cannot be sold to the general public at less than the cover price imposed by the publisher under the terms of the Net Book Agreement, there are many ways that librarians can obtain reductions in prices both for books and for the many other materials that are purchased. In this chapter we will consider these matters and will look at the various techniques that librarians employ to stock their libraries.

Almost all public libraries and many academic libraries apply to the Publishers' Association for a library licence. In its application the library authority will list the names of designated suppliers. The Publishers' Association will then contact these suppliers and, provided their agreement is obtained, will issue a licence which will allow the suppliers to offer a discount of 10 per cent off net books. There will still be some books, imported or non-net books, on which the full cover price may be charged but these form a small proportion of the purchases of most libraries. This discount is not available to industrial and commercial libraries since the basis upon which the licence is granted is that the library is open to the general public. It follows from the issue of the library licence that the library authority intends to place a considerable amount of business with the suppliers and therefore they become the library's main sources of book material.

Books, while forming an important part of a library's

materials, are not the whole picture, and increasingly librarians are dealing with organizations which are not on their library licence in order to obtain audio-visual materials, and in some cases are dealing with galleries for the purchase of photographs and works of art. It it unusual in these days to find even the smallest library dealing with a single supplier for all its library requirements. Consequently, the skill of shopping around and assessing the cost-effectiveness of a supplier's goods and services is important for the librarian to develop.

Stock selection

Having looked in some detail at actual library stock and its presentation we can turn to the consideration of how it was selected in the first place.

Most librarians use a variety of sources of information, some we shall look at in greater detail when we consider the 'effective use of library materials' (chapter 8, page 132), but at this stage it is sufficient to recognize that stock selection is done on a planned and logical basis. It is *not* done on whim or individual likes or dislikes.

The stock must be selected to fit the aims and objectives of the particular library and so a strategy of stock acquisition is followed which will include reference to a number of sources. These will include:

1   Bibliographic record, eg
    1.1 *British National Bibliography*
    1.2 *Bookseller*
    1.3 *Cumulative Book List*
    1.4 *Books in Print* (British and American)

2   Review publications, eg
    2.1 *British Book News*
    2.2 *Books and Bookmen*
    2.3 Newspaper and journal reviewing
        2.3.1 *New Musical Express*
        2.3.2 *Times Literary Supplement*
        2.3.3 *Daily Telegraph*
        2.3.4 *Guardian*, etc

3   Specialist journals, eg
    3.1 *Library Association Record*

3.2 *NATFHE Journal*

3.3 Journals associated with particular subjects

4 Visits to bookshops and exhibitions and specialist suppliers

5 Publishers' lists and announcement cards

6 Subject knowledge of the librarian and staff

7 Reader suggestions.

You will be able to add to the above list from your own experience and observation but it provides a starting point for you to consider how your own library service selects its materials. Note that many of the sources will cover far more than books. They will review new journals, films, records or computer software — each of these having its place in the modern library.

The amount of information given by each source of selection, and the weight a librarian attaches to each, varies considerably. For example a review in a learned journal by a respected expert in the field must have more influence than a description carried on a publisher's announcement card. Obviously the latter has been written to sell the title as well as inform the selector!

Sometimes the classification number given by the BNB helps explain an ambiguous title and this again aids selection.

Other factors we take into account are such things as the publisher's reputation, the author's previous publications or subject knowledge, the series under which it is published and, of course, public demand for the item.

In a way we have two types of pressure when selecting:

1 *Stock building*

The aim here is to predict what our members will want on various topics and at what level of knowledge the provision should be made. In many libraries the first part is easier than the second. Subjects tend to be defined by historical use or areas of known interest, but levels are more difficult. Public libraries have to cope with a whole range of abilities, industrial libraries may only need research level, etc.

2 *Meeting requests*

Particularly in public libraries many items are purchased because a member puts in a 'request'. Some libraries do put limits on what may be requested, others will consider any type of material. Fiction provides the largest single source of requests in some libraries.

PRACTICAL EXERCISE
Find out, in your own library, how many requests there are each year for:
(*a*) Fiction
(*b*) Adult non-fiction
(*c*) Children's books.
Can you discover, approximately, how much of the fund is spent on requests as opposed to stock building?

Summary
1 You should be able to list various sources of information about what material is being published.
2 You should recognize that different sources of information have various levels of credibility.
3 That stock selection is done by many people, some not librarians!
4 That often quite large sums are spent at the 'request' of the users.

Ordering and receiving materials

Manual system
From the earlier parts of this chapter you will know the wide range of materials to be ordered and from your own library you will see the quantity of items that flood into it. Each of these needs carefully accounting, both in terms of raising the initial order and in ensuring prompt payment upon receipt.

To simplify ordering procedures most libraries have devised order forms (see Figures 1 and 2).

Often these forms are produced in NCR (No Carbon Required) sets so that they can be split up for ordering and recording. You will see that there are spaces for each of the important pieces of ordering information, and spaces to show allocation of funds, expenditure code line; site or branch allocation, and who wants the item if reserved, borrower detail.

Once completed, the form can enter the ordering system. This varies from library authority to library authority and you should look carefully at local practice. One pattern is to

Figures 1 and 2 Sample order forms

					Buy		Loan	

Author

Class No.

Title

Acc. No(s).

PSL 1058

Publisher	Price	Date of Publication	SBN/ISSN/BNB

Reports/Bureau	Ordered From:–	Rota

Date | Date Sent

Last date item of use

CHELMER HIGHER INSTITUTE OF HIGHER EDUCATION

BORROWER DETAIL

Name _____

Address _____
_____
_____

Department _____

Staff [ ]   Student Year [ ]

Date request made

CHECK THE CATALOGUE !

BIBLIOGRAPHICAL DETAIL

BNB _____

BBIP _____

CBI _____

BKS _____

Other – Please specify

USE BALLPOINT PEN – PRESS FIRMLY

J	F	M	A	M	J	J	A	S	O	N	D

ISBN / / /	Acc. No.

AUTHOR

TITLE	PUBR.

	Edn	Year

O. No.	Price	Dept.	Bkslr.	Rpt.	Price paid

Date Ordered	Date Received	Res'n

No. of Copies	Other Copies	00	COM	Card	

	ML	RH	Dd.	Replacement (previous accn. no(s).)
L				
R				

Thames Polytechnic
LIBRARY
On Order/Received
This book has been added
to stock

Class No.

batch up each day's orders and put them through a check
comprising the following:

1   *Catalogue* — as items are recorded in bibliographic publications over a long time scale you may already have it in
stock.

2   *Bibliographies* — to establish ISBN (International Standard
Book Number: a unique number for each title published
changing with edition and type of binding) and author,
title, publisher and price.

3   *On order file* — list of items currently awaited from supplier.
4   *Process file* — items arrived but currently being processed/
    catalogued.

With the high cost of library materials this checking is important, even if at the end of the day you decide to order an
additional copy(s) of the item.

The finally completed and checked form should now pass
to the ordering department who may need to allocate expenditure. For example separate accounts may be kept for:

1   Adult non-fiction
2   Adult fiction
3   Children's non-fiction
4   Children's fiction
5   Reference/Local history
6   Records.

These figures allow the librarian to see just how money is
being spent and later relate this to how well stock is used —
cost effectiveness!

Once costed, an official order is made out to a particular
supplier and copies of the order forms attached. The package
is then posted to the supplier and the library awaits receipt
of the goods. One copy of the order form will now carry on
into the On Order File so that future checking is up to date.
This copy will have the supplier's name and date of order
added to it. In some libraries the actual official order number
will also be added.

PRACTICAL WORK
1   Obtain copies of your library's order form — compare
    them with the ones in this chapter and see which is better
    for *your* library.
    List out the pro's and con's.
2   Follow through one order in your own system and pro-
    duce your own checklist of how it is done.

Electronic system
We have just looked at a traditional manual system of ordering. Many libraries are turning to computer ordering and
catalogue systems. These mostly eliminate the need for
paper records and long checking procedures. Companies like
BLCMP and OCLC provide fully automatic and integrated

on-line computer ordering. Most systems are chiefly based on the MARC tapes (Machine Readable Catalogue) produced by the British Library from which the BNB is later printed. Some also add tapes from sources such as Whitakers *Books in Print* or publisher announcements and, of course, entries created by member libraries.

These computer acquisitions and ordering systems provide facilities for the ordering and receipt of library materials of all types. Records of items on order or recently received are created, consulted and amended on-line, obviating the need for paper files. The acquisitions system operates in conjunction with on-line catalogue support systems, to give an integrated system for maintenance of library catalogue and on-order files.

Prior to creation of an order record, the user may search to ascertain whether the library already has copies of the item in stock or on order, or to retrieve bibliographic data from the databases. Only one search need be made to access data from any combination of these files. To view or amend an existing order record, the same search technique is used to retrieve the record.

Typical search keys available are:
— ISBN (or other unique control number, eg BNB number, LC number)
— Order number
— Author and title
— Title

Ordering

Any record retrieved may be used to provide bibliographic data for inclusion in an order record. An existing order may be used as the basis of a new order record. Bibliographic data transferred to an order record may be amended, eg if similar but not identical items are being ordered, such as selected parts of a multi-part item.

Input formats, tailored as necessary to the individual library's requirements, provide a swift and simple means of entering the administrative details associated with each order.

Various special types of order may be created, eg urgent, on approval, confirmatory. These are clearly identified on the printed forms. Deferred orders may also be created and held on-line until required, or until the necessary funds become available.

Discrete fund records are held. When an order is created, the estimated total expenditure (number of copies × price per copy) is calculated automatically and added to the total for committed expenditure and deducted from the remaining allocation for the appropriate fund. If there are insufficient funds left to cover the order, a warning message can be produced. Fund records are available for consultation or amendment on-line, under password control.

Chasing

An automatic chasing system is provided for unfulfilled orders, but individual items may also be chased on demand. The individual library may specify an interval after which any order should be automatically cancelled. Specified report codes included in the order record as the result of a report from the supplier may block the production of chasing letters, eg if an item is reprinting. Cancelled orders are held on file for a certain period and may be reinstated if required.

Receipt

When items are received in fulfilment or part-fulfilment of an order, the order record is retrieved and amended on-line to include invoice details, etc. The fund record is automatically adjusted to debit the invoiced amount from the remaining allocation and add it to the actual expenditure figure. The estimated cost on the original order record is then deducted from the committed expenditure.

Once items are received they can then be catalogued, the order record containing much of the housekeeping data required for the catalogue.

Receiving materials

The most important functions of the librarian receiving materials are to ensure that

(a) the item was ordered
(b) the item supplied is in good condition and has been supplied as ordered.
(c) the invoice is checked

(d) costings and discounts are correct

(e) total invoice is passed for payment.

Changes in price between ordering and supply must be notified so that (in a manual system) costings can be updated.

The on-order record needs noting-up and removing from the file. In some libraries a temporary 'just arrived' file is created using this 'on-order' form.

Once unpacked and fully checked the material is ready to pass for processing and cataloguing.

PRACTICAL WORK

In your last practical you looked at the checking of an order in your own library. Now add to that to show the stages of *receiving* materials.

Processing

The amount of work that most libraries carry out on an item before it is in a suitable condition to be made available to the reader is substantial. The basic elements are as follows:

1   *Accessioning*

This involves giving the item a unique number so that if it is lost the cost can be easily discovered. Remember that very often in libraries the same title will be purchased many times at various prices over a number of years, so to know the cost of one particular item is important. Traditionally this was achieved by the use of an accession number which was a sequential number. In more recent years the accession number has been arrived at by using the ISBN/ISSN number and by adding a library copy number to that code.

2   *Stamping*

Most libraries employ some form of stamping to denote their ownership of the item. This may be in the form of rubber stamping across the top edge of the book, on the title page, the reverse of the title page, every hundredth page, every plate or any other combination dreamt up by the ingenious librarian. Increasingly, the amount of stamp work is being reduced due to the high staff cost of doing it, and many librarians are settling for a stamp across the outer edges of the pages and somewhere on the title page. In some libraries the use of a metal dye to emboss the library logo or name on the boards is still used.

3   *Labelling*
A wide variety of stationery is inserted into library books. In some libraries this may include most of the following: a book plate, a rule sheet, a date label, a book pocket, combined date label and pocket, combined book and rule sheet. A book card is sometimes also added, but more often it is produced as an adjunct of the cataloguing procedure.

4   *Jacketing*
Most libraries now use plastic jackets on hard book covers and either laminate paperbacks or use one of the slip-on plastic jackets specially designed for paperbacks. Experience has shown that this not only enhances the appearance of the library but also adds to the life of the book.

5   *Security devices*
Increasingly, librarians are turning to library security firms (see Chapter 6) and the insertion of the trigger is a more recent addition to the list of items in processing.

6   *Follow-up procedures*
As we are all aware, the advent of the computer has not eliminated undue delay in the supply of goods! Therefore it is necessary for librarians to check their files of materials on order and to remind suppliers that goods have not yet arrived. Where a computer ordering system is used a simple program can be written which will enable this to be done automatically, probably starting at the eighth week after ordering. In some library systems instructions are given to suppliers that if goods are not supplied within, say, 12 months, the order is automatically cancelled and if the library still wants it it has to be reordered. This allows the regular tidying up of the official order files.

To guarantee standards, the librarian will produce guidelines that all can follow, giving such information as:
(a) The height of the class mark from the bottom of the spine. This ensures that the shelf looks neat.
(b) The location of issue stationery: inside back cover, inside front cover, glued at top or side, position on page.

(c) How plastic jackets are to be fixed: hinged so that the dust jacket flap can be used as a bookmark, fitted to boards and Sellotaped.

(d) Treatment of paperbacks: plastic jackets, lamination, strengthening of covers.

(e) The layout of the book card: author at the top, accession number at the top, etc, and the order of the rest of the information.

(f) The style and placement of issue information within the book.

(g) Where security devices are to be located: in spine, under rule sheet, etc.

(h) Where the stamping will be done, with instructions as to positioning on page.

(i) Where the accession number will go and the number of places within the book: back of title page, date label, etc.

While these instructions will form part of the staff manual they are usually issued to individual members of staff as a special aide-memoire.

Bibliography

Burkett, J *Library practice: a manual and textbook.* ELM Publications, 1977.

Grieder, Ted *Acquisitions.* Greenwood Press, 1978.

Written assignments

1 List four types of materials and explain how your library orders them. Are different forms used for ordering?

2 Outline, sequentially, each stage a book passes through in your library, from the moment it arrives until it is on the library shelf.

3 Redesign your library's current ordering stationery, and explain how the changes could be beneficial to the operation of the ordering procedure.

4 List the ways available to obtain materials at a reduced price. Comment on those used by your library.

5 Prepare a 'mock-up' of the issue stationery used in your library. Compare it with that used in another type of library. Discuss the advantages/disadvantages of each style.

Chapter Four

Classification

The basic concept of classification
Many people stand in awe of 'classification', believing it to be a skill completely beyond their capabilities. The truth is that everyone of us is involved in the process of classification as part of our day to day lives and often it is a subconscious activity.

The process begins when we are toddlers acquiring a vocabulary. Try to imagine yourself as a 2½-year-old, out walking in the park with your mum, when across your path pads a little animal. You note that it is furry, and has four legs and a tail. Your mother informs you, 'It's a dog.' Some days later, you are again out with Mum but this time at the local shopping precinct. Right across your path strides a little furry animal with four legs and a tail. You proudly say 'Dog', but Mother says, 'No, dear! That's a cat.' At that point your brain has to wrestle with a problem. 'What is it that distinguishes the cat from the dog?'

Children very quickly learn to differentiate and categorize so that they can correctly name what they see. The noting of similarities and differences becomes almost automatic so that there is instantaneous recognition, and it is not long before the child identifies a Pekinese as a dog and an Alsatian as a dog. Now he is classifying not only by species but by breed within the species. This, then, is what classification is all about. It is the identification of similarities and differences, enabling one to group together things which are similar, and separate them from things which are dissimilar.

As has been said, all of us are involved in categorization or classification as part of our daily lives and it is automatic.

However, some people are involved in classification as part of their daily work and it is for them a conscious and precise activity. Consider, for example, the work of the shoe shop manager. Take a few minutes to think about the way he arranges his stock of shoes.

The first thing the shoe shop manager will do is to separate the stock into men's shoes, women's shoes and children's shoes. Indeed, the large shop will have a separate department or area for each category. He will then arrange the shoes by style, size and colour.

Why does the shoe shop manager go to the trouble of classifying his stock in this way? Because his customers ask for shoes in that manner. 'I'd like a pair of *men's slip-on shoes, black* leather, *size 10*, please.' On hearing that request, the assistant's aim will be to get the shoes to the customer in the quickest possible time.

Imagine what would ensue if the stock were not classified. It would be chaotic. The shop assistant would take ages to find the right shoes. The customer would become irate and would eventually walk out in disgust, and for the shop manager that would be very bad business.

Classification in libraries

The principle is much the same in libraries. The object of classifying the stock is to get the book to the reader, or the reader to the book, in the quickest possible time. The librarian has to consider the needs of the library users and the way they frame their requests. The latter usually depends on whether the reader is wanting fiction or non-fiction. When a library member asks for a fictional book he usually frames his request in this way: 'I have just read a book by Victor Canning. Have you another by the same author, please?' The best way to arrange the fiction stock is therefore alphabetically by authors' surnames. However, some readers frame their fiction requests differently and may say, 'I like to read detective novels. Can you show me where to find them, please?' In libraries where many readers frame their fiction requests in this way, the librarians may categorize their fiction and group novels of a certain type together, eg all the love stories, all the westerns, all the detective stories, all the historical novels, but there is always a residue of fiction which cannot be categorized in this way. Other librarians solve the problem by arranging all the fiction alphabetically by author but put easily identifiable symbols on the spines to identify the type of novel.

Classification of non-fiction stock
When a reader requests a non-fiction book he usually frames his question in this way: 'Have you any books on stamp-collecting?' In other words he asks for non-fiction books by subject, so the most convenient way to organize the non-fiction stock is by subject. Books on the same subject are shelved together, and books on related subjects are alongside.

When a factual book is added to the library's stock, the librarian has to peruse it in order to discover what its subject is. Sometimes this is an easy task but sometimes it is quite difficult. The librarian will look at the book's title, subtitle, preface, contents list, etc, in order to determine the subject-matter, and sometimes a dictionary, encyclopaedia or other reference work has to be consulted in order to shed light on unfamiliar terminology.

Imagine, however, that the book is a straightforward book about physics. The librarian could put a label on the spine which said 'PHYSICS' and the book could be shelved alongside other books on physics. However, some subjects have very lengthy names — eg electromagnetism — and sometimes subjects cannot be expressed by a word but need a phrase. In such cases, subject labels would cover the entire spine. Also, how would one manage to keep books on related sciences such as chemistry and mathematics nearby?

What is needed is a logical arrangement of subjects accompanied by a system of symbols which represent the subjects. Librarians call these symbols a notation. Many men have devised such classification systems — Bliss, Brown, Ranganathan to name only three — but the one who is most widely known is Melvil Dewey. His name will probably tell you his nationality! Dewey lived and worked in New York (b.1851, d.1931) where he first produced his Dewey Decimal Classification Scheme in 1876.

Dewey set himself some constraints when he launched out on his life's work. First, he wanted to restrict himself to ten main classes, and then subdivide by 10, and by 10 again until he reached the degree of division required. Second, he wanted to use numbers only for his symbols, introducing a decimal point after the third digit.

Imagine yourself setting out on this task. In front of you, figuratively speaking, is the whole of man's knowledge and you have to divide it logically into ten separate subject areas. One of the easiest ways to envisage this is to consider the subjects which are taught in school. The same principle applies — a body of knowledge has to be transmitted but to make this easier and more methodical it is divided into subject areas with departments and subject specialists concerned with each area. Find some scrap paper and jot down the subject areas taught in schools. Now compare your list with Dewey's list (below) and note the similarities and differences.

It is doubtful whether your list will match that of Dewey, primarily because teachers see a close link between certain subject areas that Dewey apparently did not see, or chose to ignore. For example, language and literature go hand-in-hand in the school curriculum but Dewey separates the two. Similarly, social sciences and history are interrelated in teaching but widely separated in Dewey. This wide separation of related subject areas is one of the major criticisms of the Dewey scheme.

> PHILOSOPHY and related disciplines
> RELIGION
> SOCIAL SCIENCES
> LANGUAGE
> PURE SCIENCES
> TECHNOLOGY (applied sciences)
> THE ARTS
> LITERATURE (Belles-lettres)
> GEOGRAPHY
> HISTORY

Dewey wanted only ten main classes and he achieved that in his list above. However, Dewey was concerned not only with abstract knowledge but with knowledge as it was contained in books, and some books pose problems for the classifier. For example, could you fit into the above list of subjects the following two books?

1 *Encyclopaedia Britannica*
2 *Six famous lives*

A general encyclopaedia encompasses all of the subject fields listed so it cannot be slotted into one of them. A special place has to be provided for general encyclopaedias and all books of general knowledge so Dewey added at the top of his list a class called GENERALITIES (formerly GENERALIA). A collected biography may include the life stories of a scientist, an engineer, a musician, a philosopher and so on. Again, there is no provision in Dewey's main list of ten classes for collected biography so he added BIOGRA-PHY at the end of his list. Now the list comprises twelve items, not ten.

Undeterred Dewey allocated his numerical symbols and the list of ten main classes ended up like this:

000	GENERALITIES
100	PHILOSOPHY and related disciplines
200	RELIGION
300	SOCIAL SCIENCES
400	LANGUAGE
500	PURE SCIENCES
600	TECHNOLOGY (applied sciences)
700	THE ARTS
800	LITERATURE (belles-lettres)
900	GENERAL GEOGRAPHY & HISTORY (including BIOGRAPHY)

Each of the above main classes is subdivided by 10, eg

500	PURE SCIENCES
510	Mathematics
520	Astronomy and allied sciences
530	Physics
540	Chemistry and allied sciences
550	Sciences of earth (geology) and other worlds
560	Palaeontology
570	Life sciences (biology)
580	Botanical sciences
590	Zoological sciences

Each of these in turn divides by 10, and then by ten again in the following way:

530	Physics
539	Modern physics
539.7	Atomic and nuclear physics

539.72	Particles; x, gamma, cosmic rays, nuclei
539.722	x, gamma, cosmic rays
539.7222	x and gamma rays

The rule to remember is:

The broader the subject, the shorter the class number.
The more specific the subject, the longer the class number.

It is quite fascinating to study the way in which Dewey identified similarities and differences and logically built up his classification numbers. Consider the chain of thought involved in classifying books on soccer at 796.334, ie:

700	THE ARTS
790	Recreation and performing arts
796	Athletic and outdoor sports and games
796.3	Sports involving a ball (ball games)
796.33	Sports involving an inflated ball propelled (driven) by foot
796.334	Soccer (Association football)

The Dewey Decimal Classification Scheme is now in its nineteenth full edition and an abridged edition and a schools edition are also available. Its popularity is due in part to the timing of its appearance. Libraries were looking for a suitable classification scheme at that time and, having once adopted a scheme, it is very rare that a library will abandon it and turn to another scheme due to the enormity of the task of re-classifying. The universality of its numerical symbols also adds to its appeal, and of course the scheme itself has merits which make it suitable for many types of library, particularly public libraries which have a wide-ranging stock rather than an in-depth stock in a limited subject field. Some libraries such as school libraries and smaller public libraries choose not to use very lengthy class numbers because the size of the stock and the needs of their readers do not warrant this. If you consult the classified sequence of *British National Bibliography* you will observe that the lengthy Dewey numbers which are given have apostrophes indicating where the number can be shortened.

Advantages and disadvantages of the Dewey scheme
Advantages
1   It has a simple, pure notation.
2   Arabic numerals are used internationally.

3 The class numbers are easy to write, type and remember — at least to hold in one's mind long enough to get from a library's catalogue to the shelves.

4 Mnemonic devices (memory aids) are widely used. Normally these occur where numbers retain the same meaning in more than one part of the schedules.

5 The classification scheme allows for expansion so that new subjects can be included. This facility is known as 'hospitality'.

6 Alternative placings are provided for many subjects so that differing libraries can cater for the needs of their own clientele.

7 The scheme allows for close classification (lengthy numbers for specific subjects) or broad classification (shorter numbers where less detail is required).

8 The scheme is hierarchical, like a family tree, showing the relationship of specific subjects to the parent subject.

9 The Dewey scheme has an excellent relative index.

10 The schedules are inexpensive.

11 The scheme is being constantly revised, and therefore is up-to-date.

Disadvantages

1 The provision of only ten main classes means that the base is too short, resulting in lengthy classification numbers.

2 The limitation of division and subdivision by only 10 places leads to the squeezing of subjects into a conglomerate last division called 'others'.

3 The arrangement of classes has been criticized, especially the separation of language from literature; social sciences from history; psychology from medicine.

4 There is a tendency to bias the scheme towards the needs of libraries in the West, and particularly the USA. This is reflected in the amount of detail allocated to subjects on which libraries in the West would have large stocks, eg American history in comparison with that of other countries, and the detail allocated to the Christian religion as opposed to other religions.

Other classification schemes

There are many classification schemes in use, several designed specifically for special libraries which have an extensive stock but in a limited subject field. General schemes such as Dewey do not give the minuteness of detail necessary for such libraries. Two examples are:

1 Universal Decimal Classification — commonly referred to as UDC and in use in many industrial libraries. It is based on Dewey but is a faceted scheme incorporating letters of the alphabet and full stops or decimal points. This is what the notation looks like:

    U 621.1.01
    applied thermodynamics

2 Sfb (Samarbetskommittén för Byggnådsfragor) — a scheme devised for literature concerned with the construction industry. It is a faceted scheme with different parts of the symbol appearing in a four-part grid. The notation incorporates numbers, letters and parentheses. Here is an example of Sfb notation:

    | 41 | (74) | Xg3 | — | fireclay sanitary fixtures for hospitals

Some classification schemes use symbols other than numbers for their notation, eg letters of the alphabet. Some use a combination of letters and numbers and some incorporate grammatical signs. A notation which uses one type of symbol only is said to be 'pure' and a notation which uses more than one type of symbol is said to be 'mixed'.

The Bliss Bibliographic Classification Scheme

The Bliss classification scheme has been widely praised, mainly because of its very logical arrangement. The provision for its revision has not compared with that of Dewey so it became outdated, but a revised edition began to appear in 1978. Its notation consists mainly of letters of the alphabet with both upper case (capitals) and lower case (small letters) employed. Numerals are used in the Generalia class.

History of the scheme

The bibliographic classification was developed by Henry Evelyn Bliss (1870-1955), an American librarian employed from 1891 until 1941 in New York City College Library. Classification fascinated him and he devoted his entire life to its study. He conceived the scheme as long ago as 1908 but it was not until 1935 that a condensed version was published, and 1940-53 that the full edition appeared in print.

Structure of the scheme

1 Bliss claimed that a group of subject specialists will generally agree on an arrangement and order of topics, based on the way that subject is taught or used (ie educational and scientific consensus). This order is relatively stable and does not alter greatly.
2 He believed in the subordination of topics — from the general to the specific.
3 He brought related topics together (collocation).
4 He provided alternative locations.
5 He provided auxiliary tables for compound subjects.

Order of main classes — following evolutionary order

A — Philosophy and general science (including logic, maths)	
B — Physics (including physical technology, eg radio)	PHYSICAL SCIENCES
C — Chemistry (including mineralogy, chemical technology)	
D — Astronomy, geology, geography	
E — Biology (including palaeontology)	
F — Botany (including bacteriology)	BIOLOGICAL SCIENCES
G — Zoology	
H — Anthropology (including medicine, hygiene, PT, recreation)	
I — Psychology (including psychiatry)	HUMAN SCIENCES
J — Education	
K — Social sciences (including ethnology, travel & description)	
L — Social — political history	
M — Social — political history Europe	
N — Social — political history N. America	HUMAN STUDIES
O — Social — political history Australia, Asia, Africa	
P — Religion, theology, ethics	

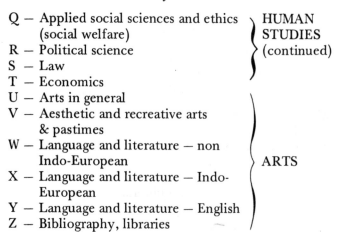

Q – Applied social sciences and ethics (social welfare)
R – Political science
S – Law
T – Economics
> HUMAN STUDIES (continued)

U – Arts in general
V – Aesthetic and recreative arts & pastimes
W – Language and literature – non Indo-European
X – Language and literature – Indo-European
Y – Language and literature – English
Z – Bibliography, libraries
> ARTS

Points to note
1 Each main class is subdivided by capital letters, eg

   B – Physics
   BC – Mechanics
   BH – Heat   etc.

2 Blanks are left for the inclusion of new subjects.
3 Each subdivision can be further subdivided by the addition of a third capital letter, eg

   BCN – Velocity

4 Auxiliary schedules
   (a) Anterior numeral classes – corresponding to the Generalia class of Dewey. Bliss uses the numbers 1 to 9.
   (b) Schedule 2 is for geographic divisions and for this he uses lower case letters, eg

        e   – England
        ed   – London
        GX ed– birds of London

   (c) There are also many auxiliary schedules, each of which can be applied only to a particular class.

Advantages of the Bliss Bibliographic Classification Scheme
1 The order of main classes is generally praised because of its logical progression, eg

Class A ends at AZ — General physical science, leading naturally into Class B — Physics

2 The placing of a technology alongside the science to which it relates is sensible, eg

C — Chemistry   CT — Chemical technology

3 Bliss proportioned the scheme to match the stocks of most libraries.

4 The scheme is a practical one as well as logical.
   (a) It was first used in the New York City College Library.
   (b) Help was sought from librarians in specialist libraries (eg medicine).
   (c) Practical criticism from librarians was welcomed, considered and acted upon.

5 Classification symbols are kept short, because Bliss used a wide base of 26 letters. Most class marks are limited to three places, although in zoology and botany they extend to four places.

Television — BOY (Bliss)   621.3848 (Dewey)
Aviation   — BT (Bliss)   629.13   (Dewey)

6 Bliss provides simple form divisions, again maintaining short class marks, eg

2 — Bibliographies   BT2 — Bibliography of aviation
6 — Periodicals   C6 — Periodical on chemistry

7 Bliss provides alternative locations for many subjects so that his scheme can be adopted by different kinds of libraries, eg three alternatives for the treatment of biography:
   (a) classified under subject, with addition of No. 4 from Schedule 1, eg B4 — biography of a physicist. Or
   (b) all biography at L9 but subdivided in classified order, eg L9B — biography of a physicist. Or
   (c) all biography at L9 but subdivided alphabetically, eg L9 B — biography of a physicist. Or
   Religion can be classified at P in a class of its own or at AJ as a subdivision of philosophy.

8 The scheme uses literal mnemonics but never at the expense of logical order, eg

AL — logic

It uses some constant mnemonics as form divisions:

1 — Reference books (dictionaries, encyclopaedias)
2 — Bibliographies
6 — Periodicals

9 The scheme has a very full relative index, which includes many personal and place names.

10 Revision is carried out via the *Bliss classification bulletin* (annual), and a new edition has been produced by staff at the Library School of North London Polytechnic. The Bliss classification scheme is now detailed and up-to-date and compares favourably with any other available scheme.

Faults of the scheme

1 The unfortunate use of both upper and lower case letters can cause confusion, eg

GXED — Divers (birds)
GX ed — Birds of London

2 There is verbal difficulty in referring to some class marks, eg GWXD, and also the unfortunate pronunciation of certain combinations of letters, eg GUT.

3 Too many alternative locations can cause confusion and prevent consistency between one library and another.

4 Facilities for revision do not compare with Dewey. Twenty years passed without a comprehensive revision.

5 The scheme appeared too late. Most libraries had already adopted Dewey or Library of Congress, and would not undertake the difficult task of re-classifying their entire stock.

General evaluation of the scheme

Bliss is the most scholarly of all the classification schemes. It is estimated that about 90 libraries use the scheme, most of which are in the British Commonwealth and very few in the USA. The users are mainly academic, learned, government and special libraries. An abridged edition of the scheme for school use was published in 1967 by the School Library Association and a revised full edition (2nd) commenced publication in 1977.

The Library of Congress Classification Scheme

This classification scheme derives its name from the library for which it was devised, namely the library of the United

States Congress in Washington DC. The scheme was designed by the Library of Congress staff to be tailor-made for their own library with its immense and rapidly growing stock and with its bias towards law and the social sciences. Each main class was published separately, commencing in 1902, and each with its individual structure and its own index. The schedules are continually updated and cumulations of additions and changes are published.

The notation employed by the Library of Congress scheme is based on letters of the alphabet, twenty-one of which have been used and five kept in reserve for further expansion.

The following is a list of main classes:

    A   General works
    B   Philosophy, religion
    C   History
    D   History and topography
    E   United States (history)
    F   United States (local)
    G   Geography, anthropology
    H   Social sciences
    J   Political science
    K   Law
    L   Education
    M   Music
    N   Fine arts
    P   Language and literature
    Q   Science
    R   Medicine
    S   Agriculture
    T   Technology
    U   Military science
    V   Naval science
    Z   Bibliography and library science

The main subdivisions employ an additional letter, eg

    P   Language and literature
    PR   English literature

Further subdivision is then effected by using arabic numerals, in arithmetical sequence from one digit to four digits in length, eg

    PN   6511 Oriental proverbs

To achieve very specific classification the class mark can be lengthened further by adding decimal points or full stops followed by additional letters and numbers, eg

PN 6519.C5 Chinese proverbs

The arrangement of stock within the Library of Congress is made even more precise by using call numbers. A call number is a symbol combining the class mark and an author symbol. The latter is usually the initial letter of the author's surname followed by one or two numerals.

Despite the fact that the Library of Congress Classification Scheme was designed for one particular library, it has been adopted by many libraries, particularly in the United States, but also some in the United Kingdom.

Features common to classification schemes
To be of maximum benefit to the classifier, classification schemes need to include the following features:
1   Schedules
2   An index
3   Notation
4   Tables including (a) standard subdivisions (form divisions); (b) an areas table
5   A form class
6   A generalities class

1   Schedules
The term 'schedules' is used to describe the printed list of all the main classes, divisions and subdivisions of the classification scheme. The schedules provide a logical arrangement of all the subjects encompassed by the classification scheme, this arrangement usually being hierarchical, ie showing the relationship of specific subjects to their parent subject. The relevant classification symbol is shown against each subject.

2   Index
The index to the classification scheme is an alphabetical list of all the subjects encompassed by the scheme, with the relevant class mark shown against each subject. There are two types of index:

(a)   *A relative index* includes broad topics in its alphabetical arrangement, but indented below the broad subject heading is a list of all the aspects of the subject. The Dewey Decimal Classification Scheme has an excellent relative index, eg

Flight
  guides
    aeronautics   629.13254
  instrumentation
    aircraft eng.   629.1352
  into Egypt
    Christian doctrines   232.926

(b)   *A specific index* lists specific subjects in a precise alphabetical sequence. It does not indent lists of related topics under broad subject headings. The following is an example from *Encyclopaedia Britannica:*

flight, history of
flight, natural
Flight into Egypt
Flight of the Bumble Bee

Brown's Subject Classification Scheme has a specific index.

3   *Notation*
The notation is the system of symbols used to represent the terms encompassed by the classification scheme. The notation can be 'pure' — ie using one type of symbol only — or 'mixed' — ie using more than one kind of symbol. A pure notation would normally involve only letters of the alphabet or only numerals. A mixed notation would normally utilize both letters and numerals. Some notations also involve the use of grammatical signs or mathematical symbols.

The notation usually appears on the spines of library books to facilitate shelving and to ensure that each book is in its correct place. The notation is also shown on catalogue entries to help the staff and public to retrieve books quickly. It therefore serves as

(a)   a link between the index and the schedules of a classification scheme, and

(b)   a link between the library catalogues and the shelves.

4   *Tables*

The tables of a classification scheme are additional to the schedules and provide lists of symbols which can be added to class marks to make them more specific and precise. Probably the most important of the tables is the

(a)   *Table of standard subdivisions or form divisions* which lists symbols which can be added to class marks to denote the form of arrangement or method of treatment of a book's subject. The following is an abbreviated list of standard subdivisions from the Dewey Decimal Classification Scheme,. nineteenth full edition:

01   Philosophy and theory
02   Miscellany
03   Dictionaries, encyclopaedias and concordances
04   Special topics of general applicability
05   Serial publications
06   Organizations and management
07   Study and teaching
08   History and description of the subject among groups of persons
09   Historical and geographical treatment

The rule to remember is that a book must first be given a class mark which represents its subject content and then the appropriate symbol from the table of standard subdivisions is added to that class mark to denote the form or treatment of that subject, eg

| Medicine | − 610 |
| Medical dictionary | − 610.3 (ie 610 + 03) |

(b)   *Areas table:* this lists symbols which can be added to class marks to indicate the particular geographical area − eg continent, country, state, county, etc − to which a book's subject is restricted. Again, a book would be classified first by subject and then by area. Examples from the Dewey scheme would be:

Cricket	796.358
Historical and geographical treatment	09
Essex (from area table)	426 7
Cricket in Essex	796.358094267

The other tables in the Dewey scheme are:

Table 3 — Subdivisions of individual literatures
Table 4 — Subdivisions of individual languages
Table 5 — Racial, ethnic, national groups
Table 6 — Languages
Table 7 — Persons

5 *Form class*
A form class makes provision for those books where form is of greater importance than subject. Most books of this kind are literary works — fiction, poetry, plays, for example. Poetry is primarily read for its own sake and not because the poems may be about animals or trees or whatever. Dewey's literature class is an example of a form class except that the class is divided first by language and then by form:

820   English literature
821   English poetry
822   English drama
823   English fiction
        etc

6 *A generalities class*
This class caters primarily for books of general knowledge which could not be allocated to any particular subject class because of their pervasive subject coverage. In some respects, a generalities class is also a form class because general bibliographies, general encyclopaedias, general periodicals, etc would be encompassed in it.

Class 000 of Dewey is a generalities class.

The arrangement of stock in libraries

A library will arrange its stock according to the classification scheme in use in that library. If a library is using the Dewey scheme, its stock will be arranged on the shelves in a numerical sequence from 000 to 999 and its decimal placings. However, libraries may introduce modifications to this arrangement:

1 *Broken order*
This term is applied when a library deviates from the arrangement of its chosen classification scheme. For example, Dewey provides a place in the literature class

for current English fiction (823.91) but many libraries elect not to use that classification but to arrange the fiction stock quite separately from the non-fiction and in alphabetical rather than classified order. Libraries may also choose to modify the specified arrangements when dealing with biography or special collections.

2 *Parallel arrangement*

A library will sometimes have more than one sequence of non-fiction stock. The reference books are normally left separate from the lending stock and the oversize books may be shelved separately from the normal sized stock. However, the books will be classified in the normal manner but will form two additional and parallel sequences to the main stock. Symbols will preface the class marks on the spine and catalogue entries to make this apparent to the library user. Reference books are usually identifiable by the letter 'R' or abbreviation 'Ref', and oversize books by the letters 'q' for quarto or 'f' for folio.

A retrospective view

Fixed location

Before bibliographic (book) classification schemes such as Dewey's became available, libraries had to use some other method of arranging stock. Some of the very early libraries did attempt a crude form of categorization but it was not systematic. The first public libraries operated a system known as 'fixed location' whereby each book as it was added to stock was allocated a specific place on a particular shelf and it was given a location symbol. The symbol related to the shelf and bookcase and had nothing at all to do with the book's subject. It was really akin to arrangement by accession number and not classification at all.

Closed access

Allied to fixed location was a system known as 'closed access' whereby the reader was allowed to approach the library counter but prevented from going to the bookshelves. He had to request what he wanted and the library staff had to search the shelves for it.

Obviously, there were drawbacks to the closed access system and we can draw an analogy from the world of commerce in order to understand them. Imagine you are shopping in the village grocer's shop. You stand behind the counter with your shopping list and, item by item, you tell the assistant what you want. He retrieves the goods from his shelves and you put them in your basket and pay for them. However, you decide next time to go to the supermarket for your week's groceries. You collect a trolley on the way in and off you go round the laden shelves. You may still have your shopping list as a reminder but as you wheel your trolley along you see a new product in very attractive packaging. 'I'll try that', you say to yourself, and into the trolley it goes. You see another item and begin to wonder whether you have any in the cupboard at home. 'I'd better take a tin, just in case', and it, too, goes into the trolley. When you arrive at the check-out desk you have a laden trolley and many more items than on your shopping list.

The situation in libraries was and is much the same. Under the old 'closed access' system, only a limited number of books were ever borrowed. Really nice books sat on the shelves gathering dust. What a waste of resources and public money! When open access was introduced and people were allowed to browse and select their own books they, too, borrowed more than the particular book they had on their reading list. As they made a bee-line for their favourite section their eye was attracted by books on other subjects and by different authors. The reader benefited because his horizons were widened and he read more. The library benefited also because issue statistics went up. However, fixed location could not survive when open access was introduced. It became imperative that books be arranged to make it easy for the reader to find what he wanted. If he was interested in gardening books he wanted to see them all in one place, not scattered all over the library. This is what made classification so important.

Bibliography

Classification
Bakewell, K G B *Classification and indexing practice.* London, Bingley, 1978.
Bliss, H E *Bliss bibliographic classification.* Class I, 2nd ed. London, Butterworth, 1978. Class H, 2nd rev. ed. London, Butterworth, 1981.

Dewey decimal classification and relative index. 19th ed. Forest Press, 1979.

Dewey decimal classification and relative index. 11th abridged ed. Forest Press 1979.

Elrod, J M *Classification.* 3rd ed. Scarecrow Press, 1981.

Maltby, A *The case for Bliss.* London, Bingley, 1979.

Maltby, A *Sayers' manual of classification.* 5th ed. London, Deutsch, 1975.

For an extensive bibliography of classification see Richmond, P A 'Reading list in classification theory'. *Library Resources and Technical Services* 16 (3) Summer 1972. 364:82.

Assignments – classification

Practical
1 Visit your local public library and locate:
   (a) the fiction stock
   (b) the non-fiction lending stock
   (c) the reference books
   (d) the oversize stock

Written
1 Prepare a written guide for a new library member which explains the arrangement of stock in the library in which you work or of which you are a member.
2 Compile a list, from memory, of the ten main classes of the Dewey Decimal Classification scheme.
3 What is the purpose of classification? What schemes are available to the public librarian? Evaluate one scheme for use in a large municipal library.
4 What principles and/or features have most bibliographical classification schemes in common?
5 What steps should be taken to ensure that the arrangement of books in a children's library is clear to users?
6 Compare and contrast the following pairs of terms:
   (a) Specific index and relative index
   (b) Form class and form divisions (ie common sub-divisions).

Chapter Five

Cataloguing and indexing

In the previous chapter, it was shown that user needs determine the most effective way to arrange the stock of a library. Similarly, the information required by library members and staff determines the type of catalogue provided, the number and kinds of catalogue entries included, and the amount of information on each entry.

Typical questions posed by readers include the following:

— Does the library have any books by a given author? Which books are they? Where are they shelved?

— Does the library have a particular book of which the author and/or the title is known?

— Does the library have any books on a specified subject? Which books are they and where are they shelved?

The library staff cannot rely on memory to answer these questions. A tool must be provided which can supply the answers accurately and quickly, and that tool is the library catalogue.

Types of catalogue
The two main types of library catalogue are:
1   a classified catalogue
2   a dictionary catalogue.

1   *Classified catalogue*
A classified catalogue consists of three sequences:

(*a*)   *Subject index* — an alphabetical list of subjects covered by the library's stock, and against each subject is shown the appropriate classification symbol. A typical example from a library which uses the Dewey system might be:

Physics   530

The subject index gives no information about particular titles or authors, nor how many books the library has on a given topic. To glean that information, one must consult the classified sequence.

(b) *Classified sequence* — this follows the same arrangement as the classification scheme in use in the library and the classification symbol usually appears at the top of the entry to make filing and consultation easier. If the stock is classified by Dewey, the classified sequence of the catalogue will be in numerical order with entries running from the 000s to the 999s. As the catalogue represents a library's own stock, it follows that there will be gaps in the classified sequence where the library does not have any books on particular subjects. Also, there will be as many entries bearing the same class mark as there are books on that subject in the library's stock, except that multiple copies of the same book are normally represented by a single entry which may or may not show the accession number of each copy or otherwise indicate the number of copies available. If Dewey is used in the library, a typical entry may look like this:

530
JARDINE, James Turnbull
    Physics is fun: a complete course for the new
    Scottish 'O' grade physics syllabus, bk 1/by
    Jim Jardine. Heinemann, 1964.
    ix, 133p; illus.

(c) *Author index* — the third sequence of the classified catalogue is
    (i) an author index, or
    (ii) a name index, or
    (iii) an alphabetical sequence.

(i) The author index is arranged alphabetically by authors' surnames, and contains a separate entry for each of the books by each author represented in the library's stock. It used to be common practice to give only brief details of the book on the author entry as this saved the cataloguer's time. Full information could be found, if required, on the main entry in the classified sequence. An example of a simplified author entry might look like this:

JARDINE, James Turnbull
    Physics is fun, bk 1. Heinemann, 1964.
                530

However, the availability of mechanical methods of document copying has popularized the unit form of entry. With this method, one master entry is produced in the form of a full author entry and then identical copies of the master are produced which, with the addition of the appropriate headings, can be filed in different parts of the catalogue.

(ii) A name index or name catalogue is one which contains entries for works about persons, corporate bodies and/or places as well as author entries.

(iii) Alphabetical sequence. Some librarians file several types of added entry in this part of the catalogue in addition to the author entries. These could include entries under title, series, translator and illustrator. When this happens, the name 'alphabetical sequence' is more accurate than author index or name index.

2   *Dictionary catalogue*
A dictionary catalogue, as its name implies, is one which is arranged like a dictionary in a single, straightforward alphabetical sequence. Each subject entry has the name of the subject as the heading instead of a classification symbol and these entries are interfiled with the author entries and any added entries under title, series, translator, etc which the cataloguer deems fit to include. Dictionary catalogues are very popular in the United States but less common in the United Kingdom. A survey[1] carried out in 1976-7 showed that 270 libraries in the United Kingdom had classified catalogues and only 49 had dictionary catalogues.

One of the major problems in constructing a dictionary catalogue, and to a lesser extent in consulting one, is the selection of subject headings. The English language is complex. Words with identical spellings may have entirely different meanings and, conversely, a number of different words may have the same meaning. Also some subjects cannot be conveyed by a single word but need a phrase. To assist him in the task of selecting subject headings, the cataloguer will normally use a printed list such as *Sears list of subject headings*. This also ensures a high degree of uniformity of headings in dictionary catalogues in different libraries. Such a printed list also gives assistance with the choice of 'see' and 'see also' references which are required to guide the catalogue user from one heading to another. A 'see' reference leads one from a heading which has not been chosen to the one which has, ie linking synonymous terms, eg

Ornithology
> *see*

Birds

A 'see also' reference guides the user from one used subject heading to other related subject headings which may be more precise, eg

Vertebrates
> *see also*

Birds

The need for references in a dictionary catalogue tends to make it more bulky than a classified catalogue and therefore slightly more expensive to construct.

Here are some examples of entries and references from a dictionary catalogue:

Author entry: (ie main entry)	JARDINE, James Turnbull Physics is fun: a complete course for the new Scottish 'O' grade physics syllabus, bk 1/by Jim Jardine. Heinemann, 1964. ix, 133p; illus.

530

Subject entry (ie added entry: unit entry format)	Physics JARDINE, James Turnbull Physics is fun: a complete course for the new Scottish

'O' grade physics syllabus,
bk 1/by Jim Jardine. Heine-
mann, 1964.
ix, 133p; illus.

530

| *References*
(see also) | Dynamics
    see also
Physics
Science
    see also
Physics |

Alphabetico-classed catalogue

An alphabetico-classed catalogue is one in which entries
under broad subject headings are arranged in alphabetical
order but each broad heading is subdivided into more
specific subject divisions which are also alphabetically
arranged. It therefore has many sub-sequences within the
main sequence.

Information given on a typical full catalogue entry

Layout	*Example*
Author	BECHTEL, Louise Seaman
Title, including any subtitle or alternative title/ Author statement	Books in search of children: speeches and essays/by Louise Seaman Bechtel; selected and with introduction
Edition statement	by Virginia Haviland. 3rd ed.
Imprint	New York: Macmillan, 1969
Collation	xx, 268pp, 1 plate, illus.
(Series statement)	(ALA monographs, no. 19)
Annotation	Written by a pioneer in pub- lishing children's literature
Class no.	028.5

Analysis of items on the entry   *AACR2*
                                                              Rule
                                                              number

1   *Author*
    Surname to be given first, in capitals, followed
    by full Christian names (forenames).
    eg BROWN, John Michael

2   *Title*

Follow the exact wording of the title page, and adopt   1.1B
normal practice with regard to capitalization, ie the
first word would have a capital letter, and also proper
nouns and adjectives formed from proper nouns.
eg. A history of the American Indian

3   *Subtitle*
The subtitle should be given immediately following   1.1B
the title, and separated from it by a colon. The first
word of the subtitle should be in lower case
unless it is a proper noun
eg Helping hands: volunteer work in education

4   *Alternative title*
Authors rarely give an alternative title but when   1.1B
they do, it is separated from the title on the title
page by the word 'or' or its equivalent. In cataloguing, the alternative title is separated from
the title first by a comma, then the word 'or'
followed by a comma. The first word of the
alternative title should start with a capital letter.
eg Twelfth night, or, What you will

5   *Author statement*
(Statement of responsibility)   1.1F
In full cataloguing the author's name follows
the title (or alternative title or subtitle, if there
is one) provided the information appears
prominently in the book) and should be
separated from it by an oblique line. Give the
author's name as it appears on the title page.
If the author's name does not appear on the
title page it should be included in the author
statement but in square brackets.
eg The library in education/by R G Ralph
Twelfth night, or, What you will/by William
Shakespeare

Author statement in cases of joint or shared
authorship
Name joint authors, collaborators or contribu-

tors up to a maximum of *three*. When there are
more than three, mention the first named only,
followed by the mark of omission (. . .), followed
by the words 'et al.' in parentheses. The names
of the others should be mentioned in the annotation.

Note: only one author is to be mentioned in the
heading, he being the one mainly responsible for
the authorship of the work. When authors share
equal responsibility, the one first named on the
title page is the one to be shown in the heading.
When there are more than three collaborators
sharing equal responsibility for the work, then the
heading must be under *title*.

6   *Edition statement*
     (Edition area)   1.2B
     The edition is always stated if given in the book.
     In practice this means that the edition is stated if
     it is the second edition or later, eg 2nd ed., Rev. ed.
     When a subsequent edition of an author's work has
     been edited or revised by someone else, the name
     of the editor should be given in the edition statement.
     eg HODGKINSON, Edward G.
     A first course in modern geography, 7th ed.
     revised by L Coleby.

7   *Imprint*
     (Publication, distribution, etc, area)   1.4
     The imprint in a catalogue entry shows the place
     of publication, the name of the publisher, and the
     date of publication in that order, eg London:
     Harrap, 1961. When a foreign publisher is named
     first, followed by a British publisher, both are to be
     shown in that order.
     eg New York: Wiley; London: Chapman & Hall.
     The name of the publisher is to be given in
     the briefest form in which it can be clearly
     recognized.
     eg Pitman *not* Sir Isaac Pitman & Sons Ltd.
     The date to be given is that of the edition in

question, and should always be given in arabic
numerals even if shown in roman numerals in the
book itself. Where no date of publication is given
in the book, it is to be ascertained or estimated
and given in parentheses,
eg (1892?) (189-)

8 *Collation*
(Physical description area)   1.5
This is a statement about the physical makeup
of the book — its pages and its illustrative material.
A simple example might be
321p : illus. (some col.); 23 cm.

9 *Series statement*
(Series area)   1.6
When a book is one of a series of publications
issued under a collective series title, a series
statement is to be given in parentheses after the
collation. It consists of the title of the series, the
number within the series of the book being catalogued, and it may also include the name of the
editor of the series when his name is not that of
the author of the individual work.
eg (Science works like this series)
(Music for today. Series 2; no. 8)
(Grafton basic texts; edited by Evelyn J A Evans)

10 *Notes*
(Note area or annotation)   1.7
Notes may be given to amplify or explain any of the
items in the catalogue entry, especially where these
may be ambiguous or misleading. Notes may give
further information, therefore, about the title,
author, edition, imprint, collation or series.
Notes may also be given on the scope, language or
form of the book.
eg Discusses the case for free trade
Text in Arabic
Play in 3 acts

When the cataloguer presents notes in the form of
a quotation from the book or its jacket, quotation
marks must be used and the source of the
quotation given.
eg 'A textbook for 6th form students' — Preface

10 *Contents note*
Contents may be specified, either selectively or
fully, in order to show individual items in a
collected work, or to draw attention to material
whose presence is not indicated by the title or
to stress an item of particular interest.
eg. CONTENTS : V.1.Plain tales from the hills.
V.2. etc.
PARTIAL CONTENTS : The place of Japan in
world trade/P H Tresize.
Bibliography, p.859-910
Includes bibliographies

11 *Standard number*
(ISBN or ISSN). The standard number should   1.8
be shown as follows:
ISBN 0—552—67587—3

12 *Class mark*
(Classification symbol)
The class mark is to be given at the foot of the
unit entry at either the left or right side, depending
on the cataloguer's preference.

13 *Tracings*
Tracings are shown on the main entry only. For
the benefit of staff they provide a guide to the added
entries which have been filed in the catalogue for the
same book. Precise headings for the added entries may
be shown, or the tracings may be in abbreviated form
and indicate only the types of added entry included
for the book, eg 'Ti' to indicate a title entry has been
made, 'Sr' to indicate a series entry, and so on.
Tracings ensure that all the entries relating to a
particular book are removed from the catalogue when
the last copy is withdrawn from stock.

Forms of catalogue

The term 'form' refers to the physical form of presentation of the catalogue, whether it be in the form of a loose-leaf or bound book, sheaf slips in binders, cards in cabinet drawers, computer print-out, microfilm, microfiche, etc.

In selecting which form of catalogue to adopt, a librarian will consider the following factors:

1 Ease of construction.
2 Ease of consultation, including ability to 'guide', ie providing a means whereby the catalogue user can quickly locate the required section of the catalogue just as a thumb index helps the person consulting a reference book to locate the appropriate section or chapter.
3 Facility in updating, ie adding new entries, amending existing entries and extracting entries when stock is withdrawn.
4 Ease of reproduction of entries, and facility for compilation of bibliographies.
5 Cost of materials and labour.
6 Space required to house the catalogue.
7 Portability of the catalogue or parts of it.
8 Durability of the catalogue.

Printed catalogue

This form of catalogue used to be fairly common but is now quite rare due to the expense of production and the difficulty in updating. It is in book form and therefore users find it easy to consult. A single volume can be taken to a nearby table to be used, thus freeing all the other volumes of the catalogue for the use of others. However, its portability can be a disadvantage as readers may remove a volume and fail to return it to its proper place. Compilation of bibliographies is straightforward as pages of the catalogue can be photocopied. The *British Museum catalogue of printed books* is an example of a printed catalogue.

Guardbook catalogue

This is similar to a printed catalogue except that additional pages can be inserted and new entries can be pasted in. It is sometimes used in conjunction with a printed catalogue as the cataloguing staff's master catalogue in which deletions, amendments and additions can be shown prior to the printing of a supplement to or new edition of the printed catalogue.

Sheaf catalogue

The sheaf catalogue (Figure 1) contains entries on paper slips with holes or slots at one edge so that they can be fastened into binders. Each binder has a locking/releasing mechanism to allow the insertion of new entries when required yet ensure that slips remain securely in place when the catalogue is consulted. Because the entries are on thin paper, several copies can be produced by using a typewriter and carbons. Sheaf slips appear to be quite durable though much depends on the amount of usage a catalogue has. Insertion of new entries is time consuming but amendments are easy and withdrawals easier still as slips may be torn out without the binder having to be opened. The sheaf catalogue is easy to consult, though not very easy to guide. It is portable, cheap and takes up a minimum of space. A particularly attractive example of a sheaf catalogue may be seen at Essex University Library.

Figure 1 Sheaf catalogue

Card catalogue

This is still the most common form of catalogue in use. Entries are on cards filed in drawers in a catalogue cabinet. Internal guiding is achieved by inserting guide cards with tabs which protrude above the catalogue entries, and external guiding by labelling the outside of each drawer. Consequently the catalogue user can quickly find the required entries. Initial expenditure is required for the purchase of the cabinet but thereafter stationery costs are low. Most card catalogues are equipped with rods which lock the cards in place and prevent unauthorized removal of entries, but rods can be released to allow easy insertion of entries. Withdrawals do not even require the removal of the rod as cards can be torn out. Multiple copies of entries cannot be produced with carbons and a typewriter due to the thickness of the card, but small duplicating machines and photocopiers can be utilized. Individual drawers can be carried to the shelves if necessary, perhaps for stocktaking, but normally a drawer 'stop' prevents the removal of a drawer by a reader. This does mean that a reader consulting one drawer can restrict access to several other drawers. Also the cabinet itself may be bulky and take up considerable floor space in the library.

Microfiche and microfilm catalogues

A microfiche catalogue has a considerable number of entries on each of a number of flat pieces of film which are slightly larger than catalogue cards. The information can be read only when a microfiche reader is used and the image enlarged and displayed on a screen. The great advantage of microfiche is that the maximum number of entries can be contained in a very limited space. It is costly and difficult to update, unless one also has the back-up of a computer, but this would add immensely to the cost. Some library members are still reticent about using technological innovations such as microfiche readers so it may be only library staff who use the catalogue.

Microfilm catalogues are similar except that the entries are on a continuous length of film which is wound on to open spools or cassettes, and the appropriate type of 'reader' would have to be provided for their consultation.

Computer catalogues

A computer print-out catalogue is usually presented in book form but with pages bearing the typical appearance of computer-produced characters like the example shown in Figure 2.

The computer may also act as a store of catalogue information from which magnetic tapes can be produced and these in turn can be processed into microfilm or microfiche. The abbreviation COM has become the accepted way of referring to such computer output microform.

A computer catalogue can, of course, give direct access to the stored information. If access is limited to certain specified times, the term 'off-line' is applied. An 'on-line' system allows

FRONTIERS OF SCIENCE AND PHILOSOPHY		
SEE COLODNY, ROBERT G.		
FROMME, S. H.	WHY TOMMY ISN'T LEARNING. TOM STACEY, 1970.	370.183
FROSSARD, ANDRE	GOD EXISTS: I HAVE MET HIM; TR. BY MARJORIE	920 FROS
	VILLIERS. COLLINS, 1970.	
FROST, BEDE	ART OF MENTAL PRAYER. NEW ED. S.P.C.K. 1940	242
FROST, CONRAD	ALICE ABOUT THE HOUSE THOMSON 1960	640
FROST, CONRAD	AMATEUR COLOUR PRINTING. FOUNTAIN P. 1962	778.6
FROST, CONRAD	TAKING AND PROCESSING AMATEUR COLOUR NEGATIVES	778.6
	FOUNTAIN P. 1965 95p.	
FROST, DAVID	MOTOR CYCLE CARE AND MAINTENANCE. ARCO 1961	629.2275
FROST, DAVID LEONARD	SCHOOL OF SHAKESPEARE THE INFLUENCE OF	822.09
	SHAKESPEARE ON ENG. DRAMA C.U.P.1968	
FROST, DAVID, AND JAY	TO ENGLAND WITH LOVE HODDER 1967	942.085
FROST, DAVID, B.1929	ALL BLACKS 1967 TOUR OF THE BRITISH ISLES AND	796.33374
	FRANCE WOLFE 1968	
FROST, DAVID, B.1939	AMERICANS. HEINEMANN, 1971.	973.924
FROST, DAVID, B.1939	TO ENGLAND WITH LOVE, BY DAVID FROST AND ANTONY	942.085
	JAY. HODDER 1967	
FROST, J.M.	HOW TO LISTEN TO THE WORLD SEE HOW TO	
	LISTEN TO THE WORLD	
FROST, M GILBERT	TEACH YOURSELF MANAGEMENT E.U.P. 1951 (TEACH	650.01
	YOURSELF BOOKS)	
FROST, M GILBERT	TEACH YOURSELF MANAGEMENT REV. ED. E.U.P. 1962	650.01
FROST, ROBERT	COMPLETE POEMS CAPE 1951	811 FRO
FROST, ROBERT	IN THE CLEARING HOLT, RINEHART & V. 1962	811 FRO
FROST, ROBERT	INTERVIEWS WITH ROBERT FROST ED. BY EDWARD	920 FROS
	CONNERY LATHEM CAPE 1967	
FROST, ROBERT	POETRY OF ROBERT FROST; ED. BY EDWARD CONNERY	811 FRO
	LATHEM. CAPE, 1971.	
FROST, ROBERT	SELECTED LETTERS EDITED BY LAWRANCE THOMPSON	920 FROS
	CAPE 1965 645p.	
FROST, ROBERT	SELECTED POEMS; WITH AN INTRODUCTION BY C. DAY	811 FRO
	LEWIS. PENGUIN BOOKS 1955.	
FROST, STELLA	TRIBUTE TO EVIE HONE AND MAINIE JELLETT; ED. BY	709.415
	STELLA FROST. DUBLIN; BROWNE & NOLAN 1957	
FROST, THOMAS W	HYPNOSIS IN GENERAL DENTAL PRACTICE KIMPTON	617.6
	1959	
FROST, W E, AND BROWN	TROUT COLLINS 1967	597.55
FROSTICK, MICHAEL	ADVERTISING AND THE MOTOR-CAR. LUND HUMPHRIES,	659.19629222
	1970.	
FROSTICK, MICHAEL	GRAND PRIX; ED. BY MICHAEL FROSTICK. PUBLISHED	796.7209
	FOR THE BRITISH RACING DRIVERS' CLUB BY PAUL	
	HAMLYN 1969	
FROSTICK, MICHAEL	RETURN TO POWER THE GRAND PRIX OF 1966 AND 1967 796.72	
	ALLEN & U. 1968	
FROT, MAURICE	NINEFGUE. GALLIMARD 1969	843 FRO
FROUD, NINA	COOKING THE CHINESE WAY SPRING BOOKS 1960 223P.	641.5251
FROUD, NINA	HOME BOOK OF RUSSIAN COOKERY, BY NINA AND	641.5947
	GEORGE J. FROUD. FABER 1958	
FROUD, NINA	WORLD BOOK OF EGG AND CHEESE DISHES PELHAM	641.675
	BOOKS 1967	
FROUD, NINA	WORLD BOOK OF FISH DISHES PELHAM 1965 12PP.	641.692

Figure 2 From a computer print-out catalogue

direct and immediate access through a terminal or visual display unit.

In recent years, computers have become smaller, cheaper and more efficient and consequently quite a number of libraries have discarded their old sheaf or card catalogues in favour of computer-produced catalogues.

Co-operative cataloguing systems
Co-operative cataloguing systems operate at local, regional, national and international levels.

Local systems
At local level, a large municipal library or a county library headquarters may do all the cataloguing for the smaller libraries over which they have control. This system is normally referred to as centralized cataloguing. Multiple copies of catalogue entries may be produced and distributed to the smaller libraries to match those libraries' own stocks and to

be filed in each library's own catalogue. Or, the central library may produce and distribute several copies of a computer print-out or microform catalogue which covers the stocks of all the participating libraries, in which case locations must be shown against the catalogue entries to indicate which libraries have particular books in stock. The central or headquarters library would normally keep a master union catalogue showing locations of all books within the system's libraries and this master catalogue would be constantly updated. 'Union catalogue' is the term given to a catalogue which represents the stock of more than one library. The union catalogue maintained at a county library headquarters may include the holdings of college and other libraries within the county as well as its own branch libraries.

Regional systems
The regional library bureaux keep union catalogues covering the stocks of libraries within their own region. Their reliability depends on the co-operation of individual libraries within the region in notifying the bureau of additions to and withdrawals from stock. The London and South Eastern Regional Library Bureau has produced microform catalogues arranged (1) by BNB numbers and (2) by ISBN numbers. Against each book number is shown a list of numbers which identify the particular libraries within the region which have copies in stock. Libraries can purchase their own copy of the LASER microform catalogue so they have immediate and direct access to the information.

National systems
At national level, the British Library Bibliographic Services Division produces *British National Bibliography*. This is a bibliography of new books/editions published in the United Kingdom which appears in the form of a printed, classified catalogue. It comes out weekly with monthly and interim cumulations culminating in an annual cumulation in two bound volumes. The bibliography cannot be used in lieu of a library's own catalogue as it would contain entries for many books not in a particular library's own stock. However, librarians can use it as a cataloguing tool when constructing their own library's catalogue.

For almost a quarter of a century it has been possible to

purchase catalogue entries pre-prepared by a central agency. Until 1969 one could purchase pre-printed entries for a sheaf catalogue from British National Bibliography (BNB), and until 1978 BNB sold catalogue cards. The BNB numbers for new books added to stock could be traced by consulting copies of the *Bibliography* and these numbers used as the means of ordering the relevant catalogue entries. Since 1978 the Birmingham Libraries Co-operative Mechanisation Project (BLCMP) has provided a national and international catalogue service which includes the sale of catalogue cards as well as machine-readable catalogue formats.

In 1966 the staff of British National Bibliography introduced MARC, and the system has been subsequently modified and developed. MARC is an acronym for machine-readable cataloguing. Participating libraries receive catalogue information on magnetic tapes from which they can produce card or microform catalogues using their own computing facilities, or, if preferred, they can have on-line access to the MARC computer records.

Other countries also have national co-operative cataloguing systems. In the USA, for example, the Library of Congress and the H W Wilson Company have both provided cataloguing services for American libraries.

International systems
There is considerable development in this field but an example worthy of note is *Books in English*. It may be more accurate to call this a bibliography rather than a catalogue, but none the less it provides very useful information for the cataloguer on new books published in the English language in both the United Kingdom and the USA. The list is compiled from BNB's MARC tapes and the Library of Congress accessions. The format of *Books in English* was ultrafiche, a type of microfiche which gives reduction/magnification of 150 times and which can cover up to 3000 A4 pages on a single piece of film 4 inches by 6 inches. Now the format is standard microfiche.

There are information retrieval banks for many specific subject areas. Medlars is one example. This stands for Medical Literature Analysis and Retrieval System and it is operated from the National Library of Medicine in the USA. The British Library Lending Division acts as the UK centre for Medlars.

In the realm of co-operative and centralized cataloguing systems, acronyms abound. One could devote many pages to BLAISE, LOCAS, SWALCAP, SCOLCAP and the others but this basic introduction to the topic cannot offer such detail.

Cataloguing rules

Since the first decade of the twentieth century, published lists of cataloguing rules have been available to assist the cataloguer in his task and to ensure a degree of uniformity of practice in libraries. British, American and Canadian committees have worked together to produce common codes of cataloguing practice though, to provide for the differing needs of libraries in Britain and North America, separate editions known as British Text and North American Text have been published.

Developments this century have included:

1 1908 Cataloguing code incorporating a British text and a North American text.
2 An international conference on cataloguing principles in Paris in 1961.
3 Publication of the *Anglo-American cataloguing rules (AACR)*, 1967.
4 Formation of the Cataloguing and Indexing Group of The Library Association.
5 Formation of a cataloguing rules committee by The Library Association, and the establishment of an international committee on cataloguing under the auspices of the International Federation of Library Associations.
6 Introduction of computer operated cataloguing systems which had repercussions on existing cataloguing rules.
7 Increasing stocks of non-book media in libraries which necessitated the publication of cataloguing rules for this material in 1973. Aslib and the National Council for Educational Technology participated in this venture.
8 Publication of a new edition of the *Anglo-American cataloguing rules* in 1978.
9 A concise edition of AACR was published by The Library Association in 1981. Cataloguing rules for the use of school libraries have been published. The first edition came out in 1957 and subsequent editions appeared in 1961, 1966, 1970, 1976 and 1984.

Filing rules

There are several published codes of rules for filing catalogue
entries and they include those produced by the American
Library Association, the British Standards Institution and the
Library of Congress. Some of the problems which occur in filing
are concerned with (1) initials, (2) abbreviations, (3) numerals,
(4) hyphenated words, (5) words with 'modified' letters and (6)
words with different spellings. Listed below are the ALA (American Library Association) rules which deal with these problems:

1   Initials — where word by word filing is used, the problem
    arises as to where to place initials, including groups of
    initials separated by full stops. The ALA code (rule 5)
    decrees that initials precede words, eg AA, ALA, ASM,
    Abstracts. The exception is that acronyms (groups of
    initials which can be and are pronounced like a word)
    can be treated as words, eg Unesco.

2   Abbreviations — the problem here is whether to file
    abbreviated words as they are written (eg Mr) or as they
    would appear if spelled out (eg Mister). The ALA code
    (rule 6) decrees that abbreviated words should be filed as
    if they were spelled out in full, with one exception, ie the
    abbreviation Mrs. St is therefore filed as if it were spelled
    Saint, and M', M^c are filed as Mac.

3   Numerals — the filing problem is whether to file numerals
    in numerical order or to treat them as if spelled The
    ALA code (rule 9) says that numerals should be treated
    as though spelled out, but in the language of the entry,
    eg 7 = seven or sept (in French), etc.

4   Hyphenated words — the question arises as to whether one
    should treat a hyphenated word as two separate words
    or as a single word. The ALA code (rule 11) treats a
    hyphenated word as two separate words, with the follow-
    ing exceptions:
    (a) When the first part of a hyphenated word cannot
        stand alone (eg anti-freeze, inter-university) that
        hyphenated word should be filed as if it were one
        complete word;
    (b) when a hyphenated word is sometimes written as one
        complete word and there is an entry in the catalogue
        under the complete form of the word, that form
        should be adhered to throughout, eg 'press mark'
        filed as if it were 'pressmark'.

5   Words incorporating 'modified' letters — the problem here is how to file words which include letters with accents or other modifications (eg the acute, grave or circumflex in French, or the umlaut in German). For example — should 'ö' be filed as if it were 'oe' or 'o'. The ALA rule decrees that all modifications should be ignored, ie 'ö' is to be filed as if it were 'o'.

6   Words with different spellings — some words can be spelled in two ways, in particular those words which are spelled differently in the USA from the way they are spelled in the UK, eg 'colour' and 'color'. The ALA code decrees that a uniform spelling be adopted for filing purposes, with a 'see reference' from the spelling shown on the title page when this differs. In practice, one should choose the form of spelling most likely to be sought by the catalogue users.

Some filing problems occur only when word by word alphabetization is used and do not apply to letter by letter arrangement. Some filing difficulties are peculiar to dictionary catalogues and would not occur in classified catalogues. For example, in a dictionary catalogue, one could have entries where the same word is used for the heading but the word relates to author, title and subject.

The ALA code states that author entries should come first, followed by a straightforward alphabetical arrangement of other entries regardless of whether the heading is that of a title, a place or an object, eg

MARK, Stephen	(author)	authors first
MARK, Trevor	(author)	
Mark and Sylvia	(title)	other
MARK (German coin)	(thing as subject)	entries
The Mark of Cain	(title)	follow
Mark, *Saint*	(person as subject)	alpha-
Mark (Somerset, England)	(place as subject)	betically

Indexing

Indexes were mentioned earlier in the chapter when we referred to the two types of index which might accompany the published schedules of a classification scheme. Examples were given of a specific index and of a relative index. It is important to note also that there are two methods of alphabetization — or two ways of arranging words in alphabetical sequence. One is known as the 'letter by letter' or 'all-through' method and the other as the 'word by word' or 'nothing before something' method. Compare the relative order of words in the following two lists:

Letter by letter	*Word by word*
Bookbinding	Book jacket
Bookcase	Book list
Booking hall	Book of hours
Book jacket	Book plate
Booklet	Book pocket
Book list	Book sale
Book of hours	Bookbinding
Book plate	Bookcase
Book pocket	Booking hall
Books	Booklet
Book sale	Books

With the letter by letter method, each letter is considered in turn whether or not there is a single word involved or two or more words. The gap between words is ignored.

The word by word method differs in that the gap between words is taken into account, therefore all the items beginning with the simple word 'book' are dealt with first, and then the longer words such as 'bookbinding' follow.

Word by word is probably the more common system and is recommended in all the major codes of filing rules. However, problems can occur and rules would have to be followed with regard to hyphenated words (whether they are treated as a single word or two separate words) and words which can be written either as one word or two, eg book card or bookcard.

The letter by letter method is less confusing in that hyphens and gaps between words are ignored and are therefore irrelevant. This method has been used in quite a number of reference books including major encyclopaedias.

Chain indexing
This is a method introduced by S R Ranganathan for systematizing the compilation of an index which is intended to show the hierarchical relationship of a specific topic to its broader parent and grandparent. One of its applications would be in the construction of a subject index to a classified catalogue.

Each of the lines of terms below would appear as a separate entry in the alphabetical subject index to a classified catalogue. The indexer works from the bottom to the top, ie from the specific to the broad.

The following is an example of chain indexing as applied to subject index entries for a classified catalogue. In a library using the Dewey classification scheme, a book on the subject of public libraries in England would be classified at 027.442. The index entries would therefore be:

ENGLAND – PUBLIC LIBRARIES	027.442
EUROPE – PUBLIC LIBRARIES	027.44
PUBLIC LIBRARIES	027.4
LIBRARIES	027
LIBRARY SCIENCE	020

Citation indexing

The earliest index of this type comes from the legal profession where it is common practice to cite previous cases in order to substantiate a point. The principle has been applied to other information retrieval sources, notably in *Science Citation Index* and *Social Sciences Citation Index*. If someone doing research knows of a relevant periodical article on his topic he can use a citation index to see which other authors have cited the author/title of that periodical article in their published work. He would then know that these authors were also concerned with the same field of research as himself and he could make use of their work. The citation index gives sufficient information about the source – ie title of periodical, issue/volume number and year – for the researcher to trace it and, hopefully, obtain it.

Keyword indexing

Keyword indexing is used in some published bibliographies. The bibliography will normally index a book under author and under the first word of the title, excluding the definite or indefinite article, but in addition the indexer will pick out the most important words or keywords which appear in the title and include an index entry under each of these words. Normally he will invert the title so that each keyword appears at the start, eg

British town centre shopping schemes: a statistical digest (Title entry)

Shopping schemes, British town centre: a statistical digest (Keyword entry)

Optical coincidence co-ordinate indexing

The method, known as OCCI, has been used in offices and to a limited extent in libraries, particularly school library resource centres. In such a resource centre the stock is arranged by accession number and/or by form but not by any classification scheme which would bring together items on the same subject. The stock is listed numerically in an accessions ledger or card file so that if the accession number of an item is known one can consult the file, find details about the item and discover what its location is in the resource centre.

However, one must first be provided with a means of discovering the accession numbers of items relevant to one's subject of inquiry. To do this, the accession numbers must be punched on a number of feature cards which would together represent the subject covered. For example, if one added to stock a book about houses in London in the eighteenth century one would probably need three feature cards, ie one filed under 'houses', one under 'London' and the third under 'eighteenth century'. The accession number would be punched on each of the feature cards.

One can have feature cards filed under subjects, places, chronological periods, and even under form. For example, one could have a card headed 'filmstrips' and all the accession numbers of filmstrips in stock could be punched on that card.

See Figure 3 for an illustration of an OCCI card.

If a pupil wanted to discover what items the resource centre had on the subject of houses in London in the eighteenth century, he would have to retrieve the three cards from their storage box and hold them over a strong light source. A light box would be provided for this purpose so that the cards could be accurately stacked on top of each other to allow the light from the light box to shine through any holes that the three cards had in common. This is why the term 'optical coincidence' is used — it signifies that light passes right through all the relevant cards at certain points because holes have been punched at the same places. In other words they have an accession number, or numbers, in common.

On can purchase printed pre-numbered feature cards which can accommodate from 200 to 10,000 items. The

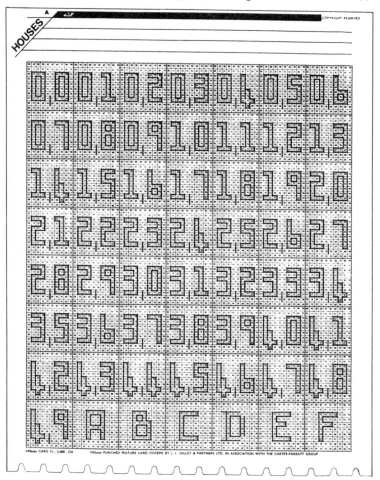

Figure 3 An OCCI card

supplier will also sell the necessary equipment such as storage units for the feature cards, a punch and a light box. Librarians using the OCCI system will usually compile their own feature list which acts as an authority file to remind them of feature card subject headings which relate to their own library's needs and stock.

Precis indexing
The acronym Precis stands for *pre*served *c*ontext *i*ndex *s*ystem. It is a systematized method of subject indexing

designed to suit the requirements of computerized information retrieval systems. In some respects, it resembles keyword indexing but it is much more precise. In Precis indexing, the subject of the book or other item must first be expressed by a string of terms which together encompass the subject. All of the subject index entries would then be shown as a complete string of terms but with each term being brought to the front of the string in turn. For example, a book concerned with the prevention of heat loss in houses by using thermoplastic insulation materials would require the following four subject index entries if the Precis method is used:

1   Houses
      Heat loss.   Insulation.   Thermoplastics
2   Heat loss.   Houses
      Insulation.   Thermoplastics
3   Insulation.   Heat loss.   Houses
      Thermoplastics
4   Thermoplastics.   Insulation.   Heat loss.   Houses

Each of the above entries displays the broader context of the more specific subject heading under which the entry is filed.

Other indexing methods are available but they suit the requirements of office filing systems better than those of libraries. For example, edge-punched cards can be used whereby the sought information is found by manually inserting rods or needles through the appropriate holes, suspending the pack and allowing the cards which have been punched at the required place to drop out. A variation of this method employs an electrically operated device which speeds up the location of the required punched cards.

In libraries, traditional methods of classification and cataloguing are still proving effective, and when these methods are allied to computerization the speed and efficiency of information retrieval is vastly enhanced.

Reference
1   Hunter, E J and Bakewell, K G B *Cataloguing*. London, Bingley, 1979. 181.

Bibliography

Cataloguing and indexing
Acronyms and abbreviations in library and information work. 2nd ed. London, Library Association, 1982.

Anglo-American cataloguing rules. 2nd ed. London, Library Association, 1978.

Bakewell, K G B 'The Precis indexing system'. *Indexer* 9 (4) October 1975. 160-4.

Diaz, A J *Microforms and library catalogs.* Mansell, 1978.

Elrod, J M *Filing in the public catalog and shelf list.* 3rd ed. Scarecrow Press, 1981.

Furlong, N and Platt, P *Cataloguing rules for books and other media in primary and secondary schools.* 6th ed. SLA, 1984.

Harrison, K C 'Elements of classification and cataloguing' in *First steps in librarianship* 5th ed. London, Deutsch, 1980.

Hunter, E J *AACR 2: an introduction to the 2nd ed of Anglo-American cataloguing rules.* Rev. ed. London, Bingley, 1979.

Hunter, E J and Bakewell, K G B *Cataloguing.* 2nd ed. London, Bingley, 1982.

Johnson, A and Baker, K J 'Practical considerations in establishing and operating an optical coincidence card system'. *Information Scientist* 1 (1) March 1970. 11-25.

McGregor, J W 'In defence of the dictionary catalog'. *Library Resources and Technical Services* 15 (1) Winter 1971,. 29-33.

Sears list of subject headings. 12th ed. H W Wilson, 1982.

Wilson, T D. *An introduction to chain indexing.* London, Bingley, 1971.

Assignments – cataloguing and indexing

Practical
1   Visit your local public library and discover:
    (a) what type of catalogue is provided (classified or dictionary)
    (b) what form of catalogue is provided (card, microfiche etc)
    (c) what information is given on catalogue entries
    (d) how the catalogue is guided
    (e) what instructions are provided to help catalogue users
    (f) how easy or difficult it is to use the catalogue

Written
1   Using the list of factors on p75 which librarians will consider when choosing the format of a library catalogue, draw up a list of advantages and disadvantages of the following forms of catalogue:
    (a) card

(b) Computer print-out
(c) Microfiche

2   The following is a list of terms in random order. Arrange
the list in strict alphabetical order
(a) by the word by word method, and
(b) by the letter by letter method
Carp
Carburettors
Car port
Cardiff
Car maintenance
Carpets
Cars
Carborundum
Carpet tiles
Car sales

Chapter Six

Basic library routines

One of the principal services offered by libraries is the lending of books and other materials. Obviously, libraries need to keep some kind of record of such loan transactions and many methods have been devised to systematize this task. These methods are known as issuing systems or charging methods. The recording of the loan of the material is called 'charging' or 'issuing', the actual record of the loan is known as the 'charge' or the 'issue', and the cancellation of the record when the material is returned by the borrower is called 'discharging'.

The charging method selected by a particular library depends to a large extent on the library's clientele, the size of stock and the need to restrict the number of items which a library member may have on loan, and whether the library has peak periods for the lending and returning of material. The choice of method will also be affected by the amount and type of information the library staff require the issue to furnish. For example, the issue will be expected to answer the following basic questions:

1 Who has materials on loan? What are the names and addresses of the borrowers?
2 Which materials are on loan? What are the titles and who are the authors of the books which have been borrowed?
3 When are the materials due for return?

In addition, the library staff may require that the charging method facilitates the following tasks:

1 The keeping of issue statistics.
2 The operation of systems for renewing the loan period and for recalling overdue materials.
3 The operation of a reservations system.

4   The monitoring of the popularity of specific materials, and sometimes, in school libraries, the monitoring of an individual pupil's reading.

The charging method selected should be simple and speedy to operate for both staff and borrowers. If the system is complex and involves the borrower in a considerable amount of effort, such as laboriously filling in book and borrower details on forms or cards, the temptation will be for the borrower to bypass the issue desk and sneak out of the library with his chosen books.

The charging methods which involve the completion of forms or cards at the point of issue include NCR forms and the BIC system.

1 NCR (no carbon required) forms

With this method, the borrower or member of staff has to complete details of the book to be borrowed, eg author, title, class mark and accession number, along with the name and address of the borrower on the top copy of a set of NCR forms. The information appears also on the other copies of the set. The number of copies in a set of NCR forms is determined by the library's own requirements. It ranges from two to six copies. If the NCR forms are in a pad, a metal or cardboard plate has to be inserted below the set of copies to be produced to prevent transfer of information to the next set of forms. If two copies are produced, it is usual to file one under date/author and one under borrower's name. The book borrowed has its date label stamped with the date due, and when the book is returned both copies of the loan record have to be retrieved from the files. This method is popular in some college libraries where students are encouraged to serve themselves at the issue point and where they do not have to wait at the discharge point because the staff dispose of the completed NCR forms once they have been retrieved from the loan files. Such colleges do not normally restrict the number of books which a student may borrow and do not charge fines on overdue books.

An industrial library known to the authors employs six copies in each set of NCR forms. One copy is filed under author, one under the borrower's name, two are filed together under date to serve as overdue notices if necessary, one copy is put into the book in lieu of a date label, and the last

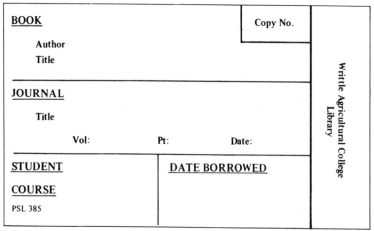

Figure 1 An NCR form

copy is sent to the borrower's departmental manager because the library receives payment for each loan transaction. The forms in a set are colour coded to assist in filing. Obviously, the discharging of loan material involves the retrieval of forms from three different sequences so it is a time consuming business for the library staff. Therefore, the method is feasible only in a small library with a very limited daily issue.

2 Book Issue Card (BIC) system

This method has been devised principally to meet the needs of school libraries and there are two variations of it, both of which employ 75mm (3 in) by 125mm (5 in) cards.

(a) The card used in the first of the two variations is pre-printed with the words 'author' and 'title' at the top and this information would be typed or written on the card by the librarian to match the book into which the card is inserted. The card would stay in a pocket inside the book while it remained on the library shelves but would be removed at the time of issue. Also pre-printed on the card are the words 'date' and 'name' so that the card can be stamped with the date of return and the borrower's name can be written alongside. A date label in the book would also be stamped so that the borrower has a record of the date of return. The BIC card is then filed, usually by date and then by author, as the loan record, and retrieved and returned to the book when it is brought back by the reader. The method requires only a minimum of effort by librarian or borrower but it does not restrict the number of items which can be borrowed by a library member.

(b) The second variation of the BIC system employs a card with the words 'name' and 'form' pre-printed at the top and would be completed by the school librarian to show a pupil's name and class. Underneath are pre-printed the words 'date' and 'book' ready for completion at the

AUTHOR	
TITLE	
Date	Name
LIBREX 35X	

Figure 2 A BIC card

time of issue by date stamping and writing in the title of the book to be borrowed. The purpose of this variation of the BIC system is to maintain a record of an individual pupil's reading.

3 The Browne system

For many, many years the most commonly used charging method was the Browne system. However, as libraries became busier, the daily issues increased and the task of filing became more onerous. Libraries which had to cope with peak periods of borrowing faced the embarrassing prospect of queues of irate readers waiting at the discharge side of the issue desk while frantic assistants fell over each other's feet trying to retrieve tickets from the rows and rows of issue trays. Such libraries had to abandon the Browne system in favour of mechanized or computerized methods which offered greater speed of charging and discharging and dispensed with manual filing. However, in some smaller libraries the Browne system is still going strong, and it operates as follows:

(a) Stationery/equipment required
  (i) Date label in each book. ⎫
  (ii) Book pocket in each book. ⎬ Can be combined
  (iii) Book card in each book. ⎭
  (iv) Reader's ticket (one per book).
  (v) Issue trays.
  (vi) Date guides (or other guides used in issue trays).

(b) Method
Having filled in a membership application form, the reader is given a number of tickets bearing his name and address. The reader presents the books he wishes to borrow at the issue desk, along with a reader's ticket for each book. The date label in each book is stamped with the date of return; the book card is removed from each book and inserted into the reader's tickets (one book card per ticket).

Therefore the 'charge' is one book card inserted into one ticket.

The charges can be counted for statistical purposes and then filed behind date guides in issue trays by accession number, author or class number (in the case of non-fiction). Whatever is chosen as the 'filing medium' should appear at the *top* of the book card.

When a book is returned the assistant will look inside it to ascertain from the date label, or pocket, the accession number/author/class number as well as the date due. The appropriate charge must then be removed from the issue, the book card replaced in the book pocket and the ticket returned to the reader.

(c) Advantages

  (i)   Simple.
  (ii) Economical.
  (iii) Can locate any book on loan at any time.
  (iv) Can locate and send overdues.
  (v)   Facilitates reservations (if filed correctly).
  (vi) Number of books issued to each reader controlled.
  (vii) No delay in returning books to circulation after return.
  (viii) Possession of reader's ticket provides proof of return
        of material.

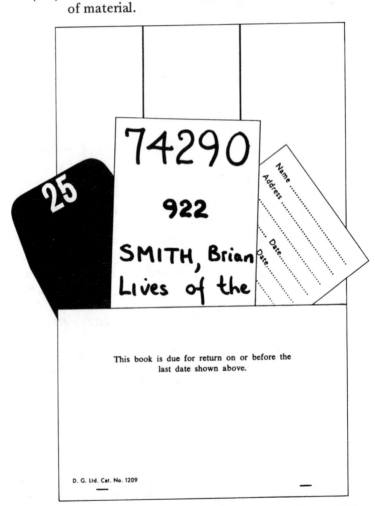

Figure 3 Stationery for the Browne issuing system

(d) Disadvantages
- (i) Time-consuming because of manual filing.
- (ii) Errors can occur in filing and discharge.
- (iii) Necessity for large issue desk to house rows of issue trays plus number of staff required to man the desk.
- (iv) Possibility of upsetting issue trays.
- (v) Discharge is a lengthy process, therefore queues form at peak periods.

4 The Islington system (a variation of Browne)

(a) Stationery/equipment required
- (i) Embossing machine.
- (ii) Plastic cards (one per reader).
- (iii) Small printing machine(s).
- (iv) Supply of paper slips.
- (v) Date label in each book.
- (vi) Pocket in each book.
- (vii) Book card in each book.
- (viii) Issue trays.
- (ix) Date guides.

(b) Method

Each reader is given *one* plastic ticket on which is *embossed* his name and address. The stationery inside the library books is the same as in the Browne system. However, the difference lies in the fact that the reader must print an address slip (using the embossed ticket) for each book he wishes to borrow.

Therefore, the 'charge' is a book card plus a paper address slip inside a blank ticket.

(c) Advantages
- (i) Fairly easy to operate.
- (ii) Can locate any book on loan.
- (iii) Can locate and send overdues.
- (iv) Facilitates reservations.
- (v) Obviates queuing to return books. One can operate 'delayed discharge' at peak periods.

(d) Disadvantages

As Browne system (i)–(iv)
- (v) Fairly expensive.
- (vi) Needs reader participation in printing address slips.

(vii) Reader may lose or forget to bring the embossed ticket.

(viii) No real control over the number of books borrowed by each reader.

5 Ticket book or cheque book charging

(a) Stationery/equipment required
   (i) Register of borrowers in number order.
   (ii) Book of tickets for each reader, each ticket showing that reader's number.
   (iii) Date label.
   (iv) Book pocket.
   (v) Plain pocket (inside book pocket).
   (vi) Book card (inside plain pocket).
   The 'charge is a plain pocket inside which are the book card and one numbered ticket slip.

(b) Method
   Each book has a book pocket permanently fixed inside the cover and on which are given details of the book. Within this book pocket is a plain pocket, inside which is a book card bearing details of the book. The reader need only insert one of his ticket slips into this plain pocket and present the book for date stamping. The assistant removes the 'charge' and it is subsequently filed. The issue trays are usually kept in a separate 'discharge room' and not at the issue desk. There is a reception desk where books are returned, the actual discharging being done later in the 'discharging room' when the charge is removed from the issue, the reader's ticket destroyed and the plain pocket and book card returned to the book. An additional 'cheque book' is issued to the reader whenever the previous one is used up.

(c) Advantages
   (i) Simple to operate.
   (ii) Rapid charging.
   (iii) Rapid discharging.
   (iv) Complete record of the whereabouts of books.
   (v) Reserved books easily traced.
   (vi) Inexpensive.
   (vii) Can deploy junior staff in discharging room, and discharge books at less busy periods.

(d) Disadvantages
  (i) Filing of charge is time consuming.
  (ii) Overdue notices take longer — no name and address on ticket slip.
  (iii) No real control of number of books borrowed.
  (iv) Reader may lose or forget ticket book.
  (v) Extra expense and effort in supplying additional 'cheque books'.

6 Token charging

(a) Stationery/equipment required
  (i) Membership card for each reader — valid for one year only.
  (ii) Number of tokens equivalent to number of books a reader may borrow.
  (iii) Date label in each book.

(b) Method
The book's date label is stamped in the usual way, and the reader must surrender one token for each book he is borrowing. On returning books the reader merely receives the appropriate number of tokens in exchange. At the end of each year the reader must be able to produce

Figure 4 Token as used some years ago

all his tokens, or pay a replacement cost for any lost tokens. A visible index (ie a list of reserved books which must be checked whenever books are returned) is used for reservations.

(c) Advantages
  (i) Simple to operate.
  (ii) Very quick charging and discharging — no queues.
  (iii) Economical on staffing.

(d) Disadvantages
  (i) No record of which books are on loan.
  (ii) No record of which books are in the possession of a borrower, therefore overdue notices cannot be sent.
  (iii) Scheme lends itself to dishonesty.

7 Punched card charging

(a) Stationery/equipment required
  (i) Computer or other mechanical sorter.
  (ii) Automatic key punch machine.
  (iii) Plastic membership cards — one per reader.
  (iv) Punched cards — two for each book issued.
  (v) Book pocket in each book.

(b) Method
Charging: When a book is borrowed, the assistant takes two punched cards, pre-dated with date due for return (both date punched and date stamped), places the two punched cards in an automatic key punch machine and punches on both cards the reader's number and the book's accession number and class number. One card is then retained as the library's record of loans; the other card is inserted in the book pocket with the date of return clearly visible.

Discharging: The punched cards are removed from returned books, sorted into accession number order by machine, and then matched by machine with the duplicate cards kept as the library's record of loans. Unmatched cards represent books still out on loan and these can be re-filed mechanically, this time in date order, to reveal overdues. A list of overdues can then be produced by a tabulator showing the reader's membership number, and the book's accession number. From this list, overdue notices can be sent.

(c) Advantages
  (i) Provides a record of loans similar to the Browne system.
  (ii) Discharging is speedy, therefore no queues.

(iii) Facilitates reservations.

(iv) Facilitates sending of overdues.

(d) Disadvantages

(i) Expensive equipment and stationery.

(ii) Charging is a fairly lengthy process.

(iii) Open to errors in operating key punch machine — really requires trained operators.

(iv) Sending overdues is a lengthy process — must look up members' register to match reader's name and address with reader's number as shown on punched card.

8 Photocharging

(a) Stationery/equipment required

(i) Photocharging machine(s).

(ii) Computer.

(iii) Microfilm reader.

(iv) Membership tickets — one per reader.

(v) Transaction cards — several colour coded sets.

(vi) Pocket in each book.

(vii) Label in each book — showing accession number, author, title (but not a date label).

(b) Method

Charging: The reader presents the books he wishes to borrow at the issue desk, and hands over his reader's ticket. Each book is opened to reveal its label, and placed on the platen of the photocharging machine. Alongside the book is a stack of transaction cards which are in numerical order — lowest number at the top and highest number at the bottom of the stack. These transaction cards have already been date stamped with the date of return. The reader's ticket is placed alongside the stack of transaction cards and a button is depressed to activate the camera in the photocharger. A photograph is taken of all *three* items side by side. Then the top transaction card is placed inside the pocket of the book with which it has been photographed. When all of the reader's books have been dealt with in this way, the reader's ticket is returned to him and he goes off with his books.

The 'charge' is a photographic record of book details and transaction card and reader's ticket. When the film is 'full' it must be removed from the photocharger and sent off to be processed. A new film is put into the photo-charger.

Discharging: If no fines are charged, the reader just leaves his returned books on the library counter and goes straight away to choose some more. If fines are charged, the reader must pause at the counter until a staff member checks whether the books are overdue or not. The colour coding of transaction cards makes it easy to detect over-dues. The transaction cards are removed from the books and put into pigeon-holes according to colour. If the books are not reserved, they may be shelved or put on a trolley.

Overdues: All the transaction cards of a particular colour are gathered together when a certain number of weeks have elapsed since their use at the charging desk (ie when they would be overdue) and the batch of cards is sorted into numerical order by a computer. Having sorted them, the computer then prints a list of missing numbers. The computer print-out of missing numbers represents the overdues list. This is first checked against the renewals record, and then checked against the appropriate film which by now has been returned after processing. The film can be read only on a microfilm reader. The overdues assistant has to locate the appropriate transaction card number as it comes up on the screen, and then reads the book details and reader's name and address which appear alongside.

Renewals: If books are brought to the library for renewal the original transaction card is removed and the book reissued with a new transaction card. Telephone or postal renewals are tedious as they involve staff in writing down on mock transaction cards the transaction card number, date due, book details and reader details. Books are not renewed in this way more than once as it complicates matters too much.

Reservations: There is no physical record of the issues (except on film) and therefore no way of recording reserved books except by use of a visible index. Some-times reserved books slip through because staff are not meticulous in checking the visible index.

(c) Advantages
- (i) Very quick discharging, therefore no queues.
- (ii) Provides a record of which books are on loan and to whom.
- (iii) Film record of loans less bulky than trays of Browne tickets.
- (iv) Economical use of staff and counter space.
- (v) Reader keeps his ticket all the time, therefore no errors regarding wrong tickets.

(d) Disadvantages
- (i) Expensive equipment and stationery.
- (ii) Possibility of mechanical breakdown or power failure.
- (iii) Delay while film is being processed (and possibility of strikes), therefore a lengthy period during which one cannot check which books are on loan.
- (iv) Telephone and postal renewals difficult.
- (v) Reservations difficult.
- (vi) Loss of transaction cards while books on loan, or transfer of transaction cards from one book to another.
- (vii) Possibility of blurred image on film.
- (viii) Lengthy process to trace overdues.
- (ix) Reader may forget his ticket.
- (x) Difficult to restrict number of books per reader.

9 Data capture systems

The computer is playing an ever-increasing role in libraries and one of its applications is in charging methods. One such method which relies on the computer is the data pen, sometimes called the 'light' pen, or even referred to by the manufacturers' trade names of Plessey Pen or Telepen.

Libraries which have adopted the Plessey Pen system have a bar code printer which resembles a typewriter except that the keys show digits rather than letters of the alphabet. On completion of a membership application form, the reader is allocated a number which identifies him/her. An adhesive label is produced, using the bar code printer, which displays the reader's number in readable form but also shows that number translated into a bar code of vertical black and white lines of varying thicknesses. The library member is issued with one ticket on which there are printed details of the library, written/typed details of the reader's name and address, and also the bar code label bearing the reader's number. Usually the ticket is made of card and it is inserted and sealed in a plastic wallet to make it more durable.

Similarly each book or other item available for loan is given a number, like an accession number, and this too is shown on a self-adhesive bar code label which is placed inside the book along with a date label.

(a) Charging

The issue terminal is equipped with a data pen to which may be attached a self-inking date stamp. There is also a card holder into which the reader's ticket is inserted.

Charging is accomplished by running the data pen horizontally across the bar code label on the reader's ticket and then across the bar code labels on the books

097 0000000X

or to :

CAMBRIDGESHIRE LIBRARIES,
CENTRAL LIBRARY,
7 LION YARD, CAMBRIDGE CB2 3QD
Tel. Cambridge 65252-7

BOOKS MAY NOT BE BORROWED
WITHOUT PRODUCTION OF
THIS TICKET.

All changes of address must be
notified to the library and loss of the
ticket reported. A charge may be
made for replacement.

YOU ARE RESPONSIBLE FOR ALL
THE ITEMS BORROWED ON THIS TICKET

Figure 5

to be borrowed. The date labels in the books are stamped with the date of return and the ticket is returned to the reader.

The charge is in the form of electronic signals recorded initially on to a cassette or 'floppy disc'. The information on the cassette is then transferred to magnetic tapes at a computer centre and subsequently fed into the computer. The transfer of information from the cassette can be done automatically using a Post Office modem or the cassette can be taken or posted to the computer centre.

(b) Discharging

The discharge terminal is equipped with another data pen and this is used to read the books' bar code labels when they are returned. The reader's ticket is not required at this stage as the reader's name will be automatically deleted from the computer records when all his books have been returned.

(c) Renewals

Postal or telephone renewals necessitate the use of a keyboard terminal. If the book is not presented at the counter for renewal there is no means of reading its bar code label with the data pen. However, the book's number must be quoted by the borrower and the assistant can then manually key in this information on the keyboard terminal.

(d) Overdues

The computer produces overdue cards which show the reader's number, name and address and the book number. These cards are ready for posting without involving the time and effort of library staff.

(e) Reservations

The accession numbers of books which have been requested are fed in manually using the keyboard terminal. The computer includes a 'trapping store' which activates a flashing light at the discharge terminal whenever the bar code label of a reserved book is 'read' by the data pen. The issue terminal also incorporates a trapping store warning light in case a reserved book has slipped through the system and found its way on to the shelves. The reader wishing to borrow such a reserved book will be told to return it as quickly as possible as it is required by another library member.

(f) Additional facilities
Provided the required information has been fed into the computer in the first place, the computer can produce all manner of statistical reports. In its initial stages, librarians tended to have too many reports at too frequent intervals. Economies are now being made in this respect and weekly reports appear to be the norm.

The onerous task of stocktaking can be accomplished quite simply and cheaply by taking a mobile data pen unit to the library shelves and reading all the stock's bar code labels. All other sources would be checked, such as books awaiting repair or binding, reserve stock, etc and then these records matched with the issue against the computer records of the library's total stock. A print-out of missing items would then be produced by the computer.

Mechanical breakdown or power failure may affect the smooth running of the system but they do not constitute disaster. The data pen system is supported by battery operated equipment, but the life of the batteries would not be sufficient to sustain the library's full service for a lengthy period. As a stand-by measure, input sheets are kept at the counter and the assistant would write down the reader's number and books' numbers. When the fault is rectified, these numbers are fed in manually using the keyboard terminal. Libraries which have adopted a data pen system use it in all of their branches and mobile libraries as well as at the central library so that all records are in the same computer memory bank.

(g) Advantages
    (i) Speed of charging and discharging.
   (ii) Accurate reservations system due to the trapping store.
  (iii) Computer-produced overdue notices.
  (iv) All material issued on a single ticket and at a central point.
   (v) Statistical reports produced by computer.
  (vi) Facilitates stocktaking.

(vii) Reduction in routine duties. Staff freed to concentrate on other aspects of library work.
(viii) Increased efficiency.

(h) Disadvantages
(i) Expense, both on capital expenditure for equipment and running costs for computer time.
(ii) Staff at the computer centre are involved as well as library staff.
(iii) The speed of service at the issue desk makes the system more impersonal.
(iv) Human error may creep in; for example, the automatic acknowledgement of the trapping store light without taking the appropriate action.

Registration of library members

The procedure entailed in registering library members varies according to the type of library. In a school library, for example, pupils may not need to complete an application form for library membership because information about each pupil will already be held by the administrative staff. The fact that a child is a pupil at a particular school is sufficient entitlement for him to be issued with tickets for that school's library.

However, in a college library, it is customary for the student to complete a membership application form if he

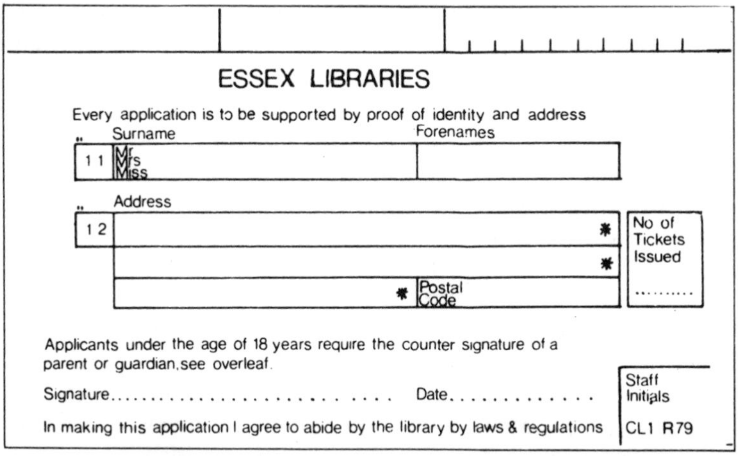
ESSEX LIBRARIES

Every application is to be supported by proof of identity and address

Surname Forenames

1 1 Mr Mrs Miss

Address

1 2 * * * Postal Code

No of Tickets Issued ....

Applicants under the age of 18 years require the counter signature of a parent or guardian, see overleaf.

Signature................................ Date..............

In making this application I agree to abide by the library by laws & regulations

Staff Initials

CL1 R79

Figure 6 Public library membership application form

wishes to enrol. Some proof that the applicant really is a student at the college will be required and this may take the form of a college receipt number or a lecturer's signature.

Proof of identity of the applicant is usually required in a public library. This verification might be achieved by checking the voters' roll, or examining the applicant's driving licence or some other documentation which will prove he is who he claims to be. The application form would normally show the applicant's name and address, and in addition a signature would be required below a statement of intent to comply with the library's rules and regulations.

On completion and acceptance of the membership application form the reader will be issued with a ticket or tickets. Sometimes the number of tickets issued is noted on the form. For statistical purposes a tally is taken of the number of application forms received and then the forms are filed, usually alphabetically by surname, in the register of borrowers. At this point, the new member is usually given some instruction in library use and may also be issued with a printed guide to the library and its services.

Library by-laws, rules and regulations

It has been stated that the applicant for library membership is usually required to sign a declaration of agreement to abide by the library's rules and regulations. The list of by-laws, rules and regulations ought to be prominently displayed in the library so that the applicant knows what he is agreeing to.

Acts of Parliament empower library authorities to make by-laws. These by-laws are drawn up by the chief librarian in consultation with the clerk to the council. They then need the approval of the library committee and the local council, and also the secretary of state. By-laws are prohibitive — ie they tell people what they are not allowed to do — and they are enforceable at law. They are concerned with the prevention of damage to the library's property and the governing of behaviour on the premises.

Rules and regulations are informative, ie they tell people what they may do. They are not enforceable at law, but wilful offenders may be blacklisted and banned from library use. There will be regulations governing eligibility for library membership, period of validity of tickets, loan procedures, hours of opening and so on. A model set of library rules and regulations was published in the *Library Association Record* in August 1953.

Inter-library loans

An extensive and highly efficient network of library co-operation exists in this country. Public and special libraries participate in the inter-library loan scheme and, to a lesser extent, in subject specialization schemes. There is also an international network of library co-operation.

An individual library will try as far as possible to meet the needs of its own clientele. However, in these days of financial stringency, no library achieves complete self-sufficiency but has to rely on the back-up services of the inter-library loan network. This is of tremendous advantage to the individual reader as it means he has the stocks of most of the libraries of the United Kingdom and many overseas libraries at his disposal.

The inter-library loan network operates like a spiral with the individual library at the centre and the local, regional, national and international back-up services forming an ever-widening circle around it. Having ascertained that the required book is not in the stock of his own library, the reader will complete an inter-library loan request form. Figure 7 shows a typical example of such a form. The form is usually in triplicate

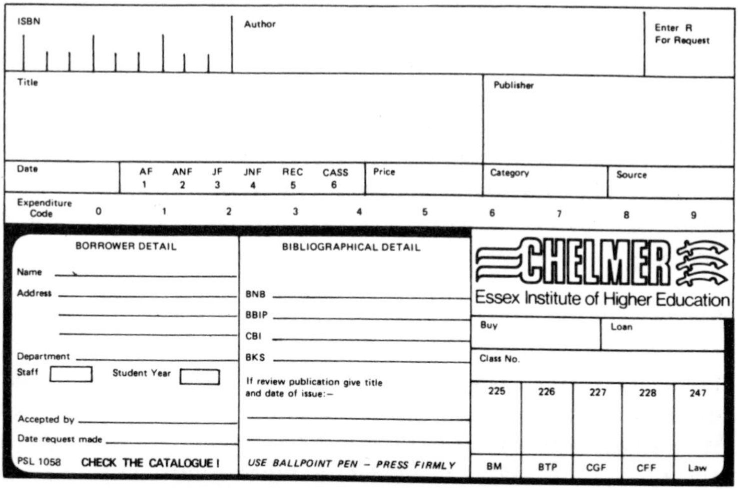

Figure 7 Inter-library loan request form

so that one copy can be kept as the requesting library's own record. The remaining two copies are forwarded initially to the appropriate county library headquarters where the union catalogue is consulted and, if possible, a library found within the county which can supply the requested book.

If the request cannot be supplied within the county, the appropriate regional library bureau will be approached. The bureau's union catalogue will be consulted to find a library within the region which can meet the request. LASER, the London and South Eastern Regional Library Bureau, has produced a microform catalogue for purchase so that the requesting library can do its own location seeking.

If this proves unfruitful, the British Library Lending Division will be approached. This is the library of last resort so far as inter-library loans are concerned. Larger libraries, such as county library headquarters, maintain a telex link with the British Library Lending Division, at Boston Spa, Yorkshire, so that the inter-library loan procedure can be speeded up. The British Library will supply the request either from its own vast stock or from the resources of another library within the United Kingdom which it will trace through its union catalogue. The requested item will be sent direct from the supplying library to the library which initiated the request. At local level, and to some extent at regional level, van services operate to deliver and return inter-library loan items. Requests supplied from further afield are usually sent and returned by post.

A library will maintain an accurate record of all items loaned to and borrowed from other libraries and will wisely provide some means of verifying the date on which material borrowed from another library was returned.

Some libraries, particularly special libraries, do not tap the local and regional networks but go directly to British Library Lending Division with their requests.

Security in libraries

Despite the fact that books may be borrowed free of charge from most libraries, some antisocial individuals will steal rather than borrow them. A library may discover that an item is missing when it is reserved by a reader but cannot be traced by the staff. However, a more methodical way of determining the extent of book losses is to undertake stocktaking of either the entire stock or part of the stock. Some librarians are philosophical about book losses and consider them an inevitable adjunct of the open access system. Other librarians feel it is necessary to take measures which will prevent or discourage theft. Valuable items would normally be protected from possible theft by being kept in locked bookcases, or in a non-public area such as a stock room or librarian's office. Their availability would be made known by catalogue entries but borrowers would have to ask library staff if they wished to consult or borrow them.

In some libraries, shopping bags and briefcases must be deposited in lockers or a left-luggage area in the library foyer to prevent their use in smuggling out items which have not been issued. Other libraries allow bags to be brought in but an attendant is employed to check the contents as the reader leaves the library. Increasingly, however, librarians are turning to technological security devices. One such method requires that each book has a magnetic strip inserted into the spine and a special exit door is fitted across which an electric signal is beamed. The book is de-sensitized at the time of issue but if a book is removed from the library without being issued the magnetic strip activates a warning signal at the library exit. However, problems can arise with some electronic detection devices because other metal objects such as belt clasps may activate the alarm signal. This is highly embarrassing for the innocent reader and for the apologetic library staff. There are systems available which, according to the manufacturer, will be activated only by the sensitized device in the book and not by other metallic objects.

Care of library materials
Libraries of today look very attractive and welcoming, unlike the libraries which served previous generations. Library buildings are now planned to be aesthetic as well as functional; in addition, books are designed to look attractive. A great deal of thought and skill is expended on the design of dust-jackets and they are works of art in themselves. It is therefore one of the librarians's prime tasks to preserve the attractiveness of the stock for as long as possible.

The availability of plastic sleeves or jackets has simplified the task of protecting and preserving the paper dust-jackets. The principle on which they work is to slip the paper jacket between a layer of clear plastic and an attached paper backing sheet. This is then folded over to fit the paper jacket and fastened securely around the book's casing. The plastic sleeving material can be purchased either in continuous rolls of varying widths from which lengths can be cut or in flat sleeves of graded widths which are ready for use without cutting.

Another means of preserving books is to increase the strength of the casings by use of special reinforcing tape available from library suppliers. Libraries may also purchase books in specially reinforced bindings, and publishers sometimes produce library editions, particularly of reference works, which will cope with the frequent handling expected in library use.

Other library materials must be suitably treated at the outset to prolong life and fortunately many products are marketed which aid the librarian in this task. For example, one can purchase clear, adhesive plastic film for covering paperback books, laminating materials for covering illustrations and maps, and perspex covers for the protection of current issues of periodicals. The right kind of storage methods must also be used for the various types of library materials so that, as far as possible, the librarian prevents damage while still encouraging use. Very rare and fragile materials will, of course, be given extra care and protection and will often be housed in non-public areas to restrict handling.

It is important that library materials are handled with care throughout their life and several rules should be observed:

1   make use of book supports on shelves to prevent books toppling over or falling to the floor;
2   do not pull a book from the shelf by forcefully tugging the top of the spine;
3   do not suspend a book by holding its casing only;
4   do not force a book open, especially when it is new;
5   do not turn down the corners of pages to mark one's place;
6   do not write or scribble in books or otherwise deface them.

Sheer common sense ought to be sufficient to guide people in the correct handling of library materials but damage is often caused by carelessness and negligence. However, with the best will in the world, accidents sometimes happen and a book is dropped, or falls into the hands of a young child or puppy. The library staff must then take steps to remedy the damage.

Simple repairs can be undertaken by library staff and special materials are available for purchase from library suppliers. Torn pages may be repaired by using special transparent tapes obtainable from library suppliers. These tapes effect a permanent repair and do not discolour, but ordinary cellulose tapes such as Sellotape are not suitable for this purpose as they dry out, become discoloured and brittle, and cannot be removed without lifting a layer of paper and text. Cloth tapes may be used to repair damaged spines or to attach a casing which has become loose.

Years ago, many libraries had their own binderies equipped with simple stitching presses, guillotines, etc. For many years, however, librarians have made use of several firms of library binders who make an excellent job of rebinding damaged library books. They used to provide a choice of coverings such as cloth or rexine, and rebound books were clearly recognizable on library shelves. Now they can incorporate the book's paper dust-jacket into the binding so that the book's appearance is as good as new. Of course, the library has to submit the dust-jacket with the book. However, binding costs have risen in recent years and fewer books are being rebound. It was also common practice to have sets of periodicals bound but, in the interests of economy, many librarians now keep back issues in plastic or manilla storage boxes.

The decision to have a book bound will be taken only if:

1   The physical condition of the book warrants binding. If pages are missing, or are badly torn or defaced, it is pointless having the life of the book prolonged. The margins must also be adequate as the binding process will reduce them.

2   The information in the book is still relevant. If the text is out of date it is foolish to bind the book. One may be able to purchase a new edition of the same book or another, more recent book on the same subject.

3   The book is still in demand. The amount of wear and tear in itself may be indicative of a book's popularity, but in addition some issue systems will enable staff to see how often and how recently a book has been borrowed.

Books to be bound are normally sorted by size because the machinery in library binding firms is so designed. The relevant issue stationery is sent to the bindery so that the bound books are ready for the shelves when they are returned.

Very specific binding instructions may be sent with the consignment, especially if the book or set of periodicals is one of a series which has been bound previously and there is need for uniformity of colour, style and lettering. A binding list would normally be completed to show authors, titles, classification symbols, etc. One copy would accompany the consignment of books and a second copy be retained as the library's own record of what had been sent. The list would be checked when the books were returned from the bindery. If the library maintained an accessions register, the fact that particular books had been bound would be recorded against their entries and the date and price of binding shown.

Binding procedure

To bind a book, or rebind it, the following steps would be followed:

1 Check that the book is complete, ie no pages missing. It is possible to photocopy a page of another copy to replace the missing one. Clean and repair pages if necessary.
2 Remove the book's casing.
3 Take the book apart so that the constituent sections are separated.
4 Assemble the sections in the correct order and sew them together over tapes or cords. Incorporate new endpapers.
5 Gently round the spine and then glue a piece of gauze over the spine to overlap slightly at each side.
6 Assemble the book cover with three pieces of cardboard (front board, spine and back board) glued to a covering material.
7 Attach the cover to the book, firmly fixing the tapes or cords and gluing endpapers to the front and back boards.
8 Do the gold tooling or lettering of the spine and front cover to show author and title. The binder will also put the classification symbol on the spine if instructed to do so.

Withdrawal and disposal of library materials

Library materials may be discarded when they are in poor physical condition, beyond repair and unfit for binding, or

Date Sent	DUNN & WILSON LTD., FALKIRK Periodical and Reference Binding				
No. of Vols. sent:		Code*	Item*	Rub No.*	
Lettering				Periodical	Books
	New Title				
	Bind to Patt. Vol.				
	Bind to Rub Supplied				
	MATERIAL SHADE				
	Bind Incomplete				
	Bind No. T.P./Index				
	Adverts Out				
	Adverts In				
	Bind Covers in position				
	„ „ tog. Front/Rear				
	Contents Front/Rear				
	Index Front/Rear				
	EDGES TRIMMED/UNTRIMMED				
	BOARD HEIGHT*				
	LETTERING–GOLD/FOIL				
	LEATHER T.P.–SHADE				
	Other Instructions:				
	*For Bindery use only				
	PRICE:—				

Figure 8 Specimen of binding instruction form

when the text is out-of-date or superseded by a new edition, or when they have outlived their popularity. One member of the library staff may act as stock editor and it will be his or her task to keep a constant vigil on the stock. He or she will decide which books to repair, bind, replace, relegate to reserve stock or withdraw. Which of these alternative courses of action is chosen will depend on:

1　Whether the book is still in print or now unobtainable. If the latter it may sometimes be advisable to put the book into the reserve stock rather than withdraw it.
2　Whether the book is still in demand or merely gathering dust on the shelves. There is no point in trying to prolong the life of a book which has outlived its usefulness.
3　How much deterioration there is in the physical condition of the book.
4　Whether the book is out-of-date or of historical interest despite its age.
5　Whether it covers a subject area in which the library has an obligation to specialize. The life of such material would be prolonged by all possible means as there may be inter-library loan requests for it.

The procedure to be followed if the decision to withdraw has been taken would be:

1　Rubber stamp the book so that the word 'withdrawn' clearly appears on it.
2　Remove the issue stationery.
3　Ensure that all catalogue entries pertaining to the book are removed if it is the last or only copy. The tracings on the main entry will direct the staff to the relevant added entries.
4　Notify libraries which have union catalogues in which your library's stock is represented (eg county library headquarters and/or regional library bureau) so that their relevant catalogue entries can be removed.
5　Dispose of the book by offering it to other libraries or selling it if its physical condition warrants this, or offering it for re-cycling or pulping.

Simple accounts

Most libraries maintain a small cash float for the giving of change and, in addition, money is received in payment of fines and from coin-operated machines such as photocopiers and microform reader/printers. Petty cash may be used for the purchase of small items such as urgently required stationery items or postage stamps.

Accurate records must be kept of all monies received and disbursed and normally the cash is balanced at weekly intervals. The records are often checked by auditors so complete accuracy is essential.

Bibliography

Advances in library administration and organization. Vols 1 & 2. Jai Press, 1982/83.
'Draft public library regulations'. *Library Association record.* August 1953. 256-8.
Lock, R N *Library administration.* 3rd ed. Crosby, Lockwood, Staples, 1973.
Modern library practice, ed. by Sheila Ritchie. Elm, 1982.
Neal, K W *Introduction to library administration.* Neal, 1975.

Written assignments

1 Describe and evaluate *two* charging methods (issuing systems) suitable for use in
   (a) an industrial library, or
   (b) a school library, or
   (c) a large and busy public library.
2 What are the main requirements of a system for registering readers? What information is normally called for on a membership application form?
3 Describe briefly the processes involved in *four* of the following tasks:
   (a) renewing expired tickets
   (b) replacing lost tickets
   (c) recording changes of address
   (d) locating reserved books
   (e) renewing loans of books
   (f) collecting fines on overdue books.
4 Describe a system for the identification and recovery of overdue books.
5 A reader has requested a book which is not in the stock of your library. Outline the procedure involved in tracing and supplying the requested book.

6   What principles should be borne in mind when deciding whether to bind or withdraw a book which is in poor physical condition?

7   List and describe the steps involved in withdrawing and disposing of books which are no longer required.

8   What measures can a library take to protect its stock from theft?

9   What is petty cash? From what sources is the library's petty cash received and how may it be disbursed?

Chapter Seven

Shelving and storage of library materials

Many types and colours of shelving are now available, and forbidding dark wooden bookcases have been banished from most libraries. Wooden shelving is still popular but colours are lighter and bookcases are more varied in their design. Metal shelving is growing in popularity due to the wide range of colours and styles now on the market.

Materials which have to be housed in a library vary greatly in size and shape from very large atlases and maps to small books like the Observer series, flimsy pamphlets, filmstrips and so forth. Correct shelving of various types and sizes of stock is imperative if the items are to remain in good physical condition.

It is always preferable to have adjustable shelving so that the distance between shelves can be altered to suit the stock. The top shelves should be within easy reach of the library users and staff, and the bottom shelves should also be accessible without having to bend double. Bottom shelves which are tilted at an angle make it easier to see the books' spines.

Shelving of books

The average fiction book is crown octavo in size and requires shelving of the correct height and depth. Fictional books of larger format are published so shelving has to be adjusted to suit.

Non-fiction books are normally larger in size than fiction so bookcases designed for shelving non-fiction are deeper and the shelves further apart.

On the whole, librarians like to keep materials on one subject together so that library users can find everything in one place. However this can lead to a very wasteful use of shelving so in the interests of economy it may be advisable to have separate sequences of shelving to house different sizes of material. The most common example of this is the separation of the oversize stock from the normal run of stock. This is usually termed 'parallel arrangement' as the sequences will be arranged in the same way (eg the non-fiction in classified sequence).

Many kinds of book supports are marketed and these ensure that books remain upright on the shelves and do not topple onto the floor. Plastic-covered wire or metal supports are designed to clip firmly to the shelf itself or to the base of the shelf above. There are also L-shaped supports which sit on the shelf.

Shelving of multi-media items

Many of these items are, or can be, packaged in such a way that they will sit happily alongside the book stock. It makes sound sense to house all materials on the same subject together so that the information seeker needs to go to one place only rather than trek to half a dozen different areas to discover the books, pamphlets, periodicals, portfolios, cassettes and slides on his chosen subject. However, there are factors which mitigate against a total integration of book and non-book stock and these are:

1   the susceptibility of certain materials to damage if housed in open access areas, eg gramophone records;
2   the possibility of theft of easily pocketed items such as cassettes;
3   the rarity and value of some items compared with others and the consequent need for greater security;
4   the practical difficulties presented by a great variety of formats and sizes and the need for economy in shelving;
5   the need to preserve some materials from possible damage caused by dust, scratching, greasy fingerprints, and so forth.

Shelving of special types of non-book media

Pamphlets: Perhaps the most common method of storing pamphlets is in pamphlet boxes. Usually these are made of plastic or stout cardboard which may be covered with colourful cloth or laminated paper. A label on the spine of the box identifies the contents and facilitates retrieval. Pamphlets may also be stored in wallets suspended inside filing cabinets and filed either vertically or laterally. Pamphlets which will be consulted or borrowed regularly are sometimes strengthened and protected so that they can be treated like the book stock. An individual pamphlet may be slipped into a hardback perspex or cardboard cover, or it may be stiffened by laminating. Such protection and stiffening allows the pamphlet to stand upright on the shelves beside books on the same subject.

Periodicals: In most libraries, the current issues of periodicals are displayed on specially designed racks. The periodicals themselves may be slipped inside protective plastic or perspex cases with transparent front covers. Back issues are stored in sets and may be bound when the correct number of issues and the relevant indexes are to hand. Some display racks are designed so that the sloping display shelf lifts up to reveal storage space underneath for back issues. Otherwise, many types of storage containers are marketed and there is a wide range of attractive designs and colours to choose from. The binding of back issues is less popular now owing to the high costs involved, but in this technological age, it is becoming increasingly common to see microfiche or microfilm issues of periodicals. In many instances, microform editions are available for purchase and librarians may opt to buy these instead of the paper copies. In other cases, librarians pay to have their own paper copies microfilmed. Microform issues are more durable than paper copies and of course they have the tremendous advantage of taking up the minimum of storage space.

Newspapers: Paper copies of newspapers present storage problems. The quality of the paper is often poor and it yellows and becomes brittle with age. In years gone by, it used to be quite common for back issues of newspapers to be bound into massive volumes which one could hardly lift. This practice has now been superseded by the microfilming of back issues of newspapers or the purchase of microform editions in lieu of paper copies. In some libraries, of course, the demand for back issues of newspapers is very limited so it is deemed sufficient to keep bundles of newspapers just sitting on shelves for a specified limited period before discarding them. They are often stored in a non-public area and staff retrieve copies requested by library members. This reduces the possibility of copies being mis-filed or going astray.

Cuttings from newspapers and periodicals: Methods of storage employed for cuttings collections vary according to the purpose and life-expectancy of the cuttings. Those of an ephemeral nature which will be discarded within a fairly short period may be roughly sorted, possibly by broad subject, into large envelopes or manilla wallets and kept in filing cabinets. Alternatively, they may be put into cardboard boxes and stored on shelves.

Cuttings which are to be kept for a long time may be kept in looseleaf binders or albums or possibly individually mounted and laminated.

Duplicated paper materials, eg handouts: Academic libraries may stock handouts produced by teaching staff. Sometimes these are not kept on open shelves as it may be considered undesirable for students to have access to them before the lecturer is ready to introduce the topic in class. They may therefore be kept in an area to which only staff (academic staff as well as library staff) have access.

It is common practice to file a single copy of each handout in classified sequence in a series of ring binders. Each handout may also have an accession number prominently displayed on it. Multiple copies, usually enough for one class of students or pupils, may also be available. The supply would need to be replenished when the multiple copies had been used, so a master would be kept — usually for offset litho reproduction or for cutting a stencil on an electronic scanner.

Microforms: This is the generic term for all types of micro-reproduction. It includes microfilm, microfiche and micro-card.

Microfilm is a continuous length of film wound onto an open spool. A microfilm reader must be used to magnify the reduced image so that it appears in readable size on the machine's screen. The microfilm is wound from the full spool on to an empty take-up spool, via the lens system. After use it must be rewound on to the original spool. Modern machines have an automatic facility for fast-forward and rewind as well as a manual control for slower, more precise location of the required information on the microfilm.

Microfilms are supplied in their own compact cardboard

boxes and can be housed on shelves or in drawers in a storage cabinet.

Cassetted microfilm consists of a miniature full spool and empty take-up spool enclosed inside a cassette. Naturally, it requires a special machine designed for use with cassetted microfilm. British Standards are available in this format. The rectangular shape of the cassettes is rather awkward but they can stand on shelves or be kept in drawers in a cabinet.

Microfiche is a flat piece of transparent film containing images greatly reduced in size. To bring them back to readable size one needs a microfiche reader. Microfiches are best kept in individual envelopes — to prevent damage from dust and fingerprints — filed in drawers similar to catalogue cabinet drawers or in binders designed for the purpose.

Ultrafiche is a refinement of microfiche but with reduction/ magnification 120 times the original. However, the ultrafiche format seems to have been abandoned in favour of traditional microfiche. Naturally, libraries prefer to standardize on equipment and would not want to purchase an ultrafiche reader as well as a microfiche reader.

Microcard is an opaque card with reduced images which again must be magnified on an appropriate machine before the text can be read. Microcard has also been superseded by microfiche.

It is worth noting that most machines are 'reader/printers' not just 'readers' and they can produce a paper copy of what appears on the screen.

Storage of specified types of non-print media

Slides (35mm transparencies): A slide is a piece of 35mm film mounted in a cardboard or plastic frame. Occasionally the slide may be mounted between two pieces of glass to prevent damage caused by dust or fingerprints, but this precaution would be taken only if the slide was irreplaceable or very valuable. Slides may be purchased individually, in a set, or in a tape/slide or cassette/slide package, and most sets or packages are supplied with an accompanying booklet or notes.

There are several methods of storing slides, the most popular being to keep them in individual pockets in transparent plastic wallets which are suspended in an ordinary vertical filing cabinet. The whole wallet may be lifted out and

placed on or in front of an illuminated light-box to facilitate
previewing of the slides. Each slide must be identified with an
accession/location number or symbol and its compartment in
the wallet similarly identified. This makes it easy to see
whether any slides are missing. Some plastic wallets contain a
large pocket in which the accompanying notes can be stored.

Other commercially available wallets are made of a more
pliable transparent plastic — again with a separate pocket for
each slide — and these can be folded to fit into a cardboard
box. The spine of the box may be labelled so that it can sit
on shelves alongside the book stock on the same subject. A
well known library supplier produces very attractive storage
boxes, some of which are especially designed to hold slides.

In academic libraries, it may be deemed preferable to store
some slides in projector magazines (carousels or slide trays)
so that they are ready for immediate projection. This is done
if a set of slides is in regular use by teaching staff because it
ensures that the slides are always in the correct order and the
right way round for viewing. The slides are never handled,
they are kept dust-free, and they are ready for immediate use.
Projector magazines are supplied in storage boxes which can
be labelled clearly on the outside to facilitate retrieval. The
boxes will sit happily on the bookshelves. The disadvantages
of this method are that individual slides which might be
useful in another context are not readily available and
previewing is not as easy as with the transparent wallets.

Film strips: A film-strip looks like a set of unmounted slides.
joined together to make a continuous length of film. Each
picture is known as a frame. Most film-strips are full-frame
but some are half-frame, ie they have two smaller pictures
occupying the same area as would normally be filled by one.
Film-strip projectors are usually equipped with an attachment
for showing half-frame strips. Film-strips are normally
supplied in their own plastic or metal cylindrical containers,
which used to vary tremendously in size but now there is
much more standardization. The title of the film-strip will
already appear on the lid of the container but it is advisable
to mark the lid or base of the container with an accession
number and classification symbol. A self-adhesive label
should also appear on the film-strip itself to ensure that each
film-strip is returned correctly to its own container after use.

Again, there are several methods of storing film-strips. The most common method is to house them in shallow drawers in a cabinet. Preferably, the drawers should be divided up into individual compartments to prevent containers moving about when the drawer is opened and also to make access to and return of film-strips easier and quicker. Accompanying notes should bear the same accession number/classification symbol as the film-strip, and should be stored nearby.

A method of storage which allows one to browse and to see the entire stock of film-strips on display together is to house them side by side on shallow shelves, or supported by strategically placed pegs, with the canister lids facing outwards. The film-strips can be arranged in classified order with the classification symbols and titles prominently shown on the lids. The film-strips may roll sideways a little as a canister is removed if they are housed on flat shelves. The pegs would normally be placed in a series of triangles so no rolling could occur. The shelves also need a lip at the rear if they are not backed.

Alternatively, film-strips and accompanying notes may be kept in a series of strong, transparent bags suspended from a rail, rather like clothes suspended on coat hangers. This method makes issuing easy as the filmstrip and notes are borrowed in the same packaging in which they are stored.

Equipment is available to facilitate previewing with minimum handling of the film-strip. A typical example is a long length of transparent perspex with grooves at the side which is designed to hold the film-strip rigid while it is held up to the light or placed in front of an illuminated light-box.

Film-strips may be converted into slides by cutting and mounting – either by machine or by hand. This allows one to show frames in one's own selected order and to discard frames which are not required.

Film-loops: A film-loop is a length of 8mm or 16mm film wound into a cassette in such a way that the end of the film is attached to the beginning. This allows the film-loop to be re-run after projection without having to rewind. A film-loop projector is necessary for viewing.

Film-loops can be purchased from commercial suppliers. They are usually on specific topics, and are quite short in viewing time. They are supplied in their own boxes and can be labelled to sit on the bookshelves with the book stock if required.

Films: 16mm films are supplied in their own cylindrical containers which are best housed vertically in racks which resemble bicycle storage racks. Vertical storage allows retrieval of a specific film without having to lift off several others as would happen if they were stored horizontally on top of one another. One can also place the cylindrical container into an oblong storage box to allow vertical storage on ordinary shelves. Shelf supports prevent the films toppling over when one is removed from the shelves.

Films need to be rewound after use and should be checked regularly for damage.

Audio-tapes: Audio-tapes are reels or spools of magnetic tape on which sound has been recorded. They are much less common now as cassettes have tended to oust open-spool tapes. Hi-fi enthusiasts and connoisseurs of music prefer open-spool tape because it gives a better quality of reproduction than cassette. An open-spool tape recorder is required to play audio-tapes.

Audio-tapes are supplied in their own plastic or cardboard boxes with facility for labelling the spines. They will then sit quite happily on shelves alongside the book stock if required. If audio-tapes are left on the shelves for long periods without being played, they suffer from print-through. To prevent this, the tape should be run through; not necessarily played but put through the tape recorder at fast forward position.

Audio-cassettes: Cassettes are really miniature audio-tapes but with both spools enclosed in a container to minimize possible damage to the tape caused by handling or dust. The tape is therefore very narrow and much thinner than that used on open-spool machines. Cassettes are supplied in their own little boxes and are referred to by their playing time at C30 (half an hour playing time), C60 (one hour), C120 (two hours). C120 tape is extremely thin and it may stretch, crinkle or spill out of the cassette.

Cassettes pose storage problems for the librarian because of their size. They can be slipped so easily into a pocket or handbag that losses are high unless preventive measures are taken. Some librarians choose to house cassettes in display racks which are locked to prevent unauthorized removal. This allows borrowers to browse but it is tedious for staff to keep unlocking the case every time a cassette is borrowed or returned.

Alternatively, the cassettes themselves may be kept on closed access and only the empty cases left on open display, or descriptive cards can be displayed which give details of the cassettes. These can also be colour-coded to identify the type of cassette, eg orchestral music, folk music or spoken word. Accession numbers usually provide the link between the display case or card and the actual cassette.

Cartridges: Cartridges are similar to cassettes but larger. They are less popular and rarely found in libraries.

Videotapes: Videotapes are similar to audio-tapes in appearance as they are magnetic tapes on open spool. The difference is that videotapes record visual images as well as sound. A videotape recorder (VTR) and a monitor (TV set) are necessary for playback.

Videotapes are supplied in their own sturdy plastic boxes and they stand firmly on ordinary shelves. Wooden shelves are better than metal shelves because of the conductivity factor, and as with audio-tapes it is essential that videotapes are run through the VTR from time to time to prevent print-through.

Videocassettes: Videocassettes superseded videotapes in the same way that audio-cassettes followed and almost replaced audio-tapes. Videocassettes must be played on a videocassette recorder (VCR), and a monitor (TV) is required for viewing. Videocassettes can record and play-back colour pictures, provided the monitor also has the facility for colour. Video-cassettes come in several formats such as Beta and VHS but all will stand securely on the open shelves. Their spines can be labelled to show titles and classification symbols.

Maps and charts: Ordnance survey maps can be purchased in a special format for library use. The maps are strengthened, laminated and folded to fit into a hardback cover so that, to all intents and purposes, they can be shelved like books.

Small maps should ideally be mounted and laminated and then stored in filing cabinets. Large maps and charts should also be laminated and then housed in map chests. Vertical storage is preferable as a required map may be removed without much handling of the other maps. Some vertical storage chests have two pairs of 'elephants' tusks' on which the maps are suspended. Others utilize wooden rods to which the maps are attached and some use clips or pegs. It is sometimes necessary to weight the bottom of each map with a piece of dowelling to prevent curling up.

Some libraries have horizontal map chests where maps are laid flat in drawers, but there is a tendency for smaller items to be pushed to the back and possibly crumpled as the drawer is opened and closed. Also each map is likely to be handled while one is searching for the particular map which is required.

Occasionally charts or maps are rolled up and stored in cardboard rolls housed in a structure like an umbrella stand. This may make the loan of maps easier, but they do not stay flat for display purposes.

It is not wise to stick drawing pins into the corners of maps when displaying them. Ideally one should use a magnetic board and small magnets designed for display purposes.

Photographs: Photographs form an important part of local history collections. Ideally they should be mounted and possibly covered with non-adhesive protective plastic. Filing cabinets offer a satisfactory method of storage. Lateral filing is preferable to vertical filing as one does not have to lean over to reach items at the back of a drawer.

Illustrations: Illustrations should be mounted on card and laminated unless they are of ephemeral interest. They can be kept in classified order, possibly several on the same topic in a single manilla wallet, and stored in filing cabinets. Again, lateral filing offers some advantages over vertical filing.

Portfolios: Portfolios are produced commercially, for example, Jackdaws, but they can also be home-produced. A portfolio is really a manilla wallet containing several separate items related to a specific topic. The contents may include facsimiles of maps or bills, illustrations, pages of text and so on. Each item must be identified by an accession number and classification symbol to make it easy to re-file any item which becomes separated from the rest of the contents. Portfolios are an awkward shape and do not sit happily on the bookshelves. They are best kept in filing cabinets in classified order.

Kits and packages: School libraries/resource centres may well have kits and packages in stock. They are teaching/learning aids which demonstrate, through samples in various compartments of a cardboard box, the development of a product. For example, a kit devoted to 'cotton' may contain samples of the cotton plant, cotton fibres at various stages and a piece of cotton cloth. The box might stand upright on the shelves with the books if its contents allowed this. Otherwise they would have to be stored horizontally, possibly in a cupboard. The contents of each kit should be listed inside the box and a regular check made to see that nothing has gone astray.

Models: Again, it is likely to be school or other academic libraries/resource centres which have models in stock. Their function would be as teaching/learning aids for use in the classroom. Their awkward shapes and sizes as well as their possible fragility make it essential for models to be housed in closed access areas, probably in cupboards or display cabinets.

Artefacts: Artefacts are man-made objects. Examples which might be found in a resource centre are tools excavated locally in archaeological digs. Again their shape and size makes them totally unsuitable for integrating with the book stock and they are best kept in boxes, suitably labelled, in cupboards or display cases.

Realia: The term realia refers to natural objects as opposed to man-made ones. Examples would include geological specimens or fossils. Their storage problems and the solutions to them are similar to those of artefacts.

Storage of rare, fragile and secret materials

Some libraries are fortunate enough to have in stock rare items such as first editions of books or valuable manuscripts. Obviously these call for much greater security and also much more care in handling and storage. Such items may be kept in locked cupboards, bookcases or display cases to which some type of alarm device is fitted. Sometimes these materials need to be kept in conditions where the temperature and humidity are monitored and kept constant if possible. It is a problem for the librarian to find a happy medium between the need for protecting rare items from damage and theft and the wish to allow as many people as possible to benefit from seeing them. To shut away such masterpieces in closed vaults seems a very negative solution.

Public libraries rarely stock secret materials but these may be found in government libraries or industrial libraries. Librarians of establishments which hold secret documents are usually bound by the Official Secrets Act, and they have to be extremely careful about the security of secret items. Obviously they will be kept under lock and key at all times and not made accessible to unauthorized persons.

Practical assignments

1   Visit the ILEA Centre for Learning Resources, 275 Kennington Lane, London and/or the Resource Centre of the Commonwealth Institute, Kensington, London or a large resource centre in your own locality to see the tremendous variety of multi-media items in stock and the various methods of storing them.
2   Walk around the library in which you work or of which you are a member and note how many different types/ sizes of shelving and storage areas there are. Consider the reasons for their provision.
3   Browse through the stationery and furniture catalogues of library suppliers such as Gresswell, Libraco and Librex. Note the variety of book repair materials and also the range of shelving and storage units available to libraries.

Written assignments

1   Write a definition of each of the following:
    (a) parallel arrangement
    (b) lateral filing
    (c) microforms
    (d) artefacts.
2   Describe and evaluate methods of shelving/storing the following:
    (a) oversize books
    (b) large maps and charts
    (c) gramophone records.

Bibliography
Cabeceiras, James *The multimedia library: materials selection and use.* Academic Press, 1978.

Miller, Shirley *The vertical file and its satellites.* 2nd ed. Libraries Unlimited, 1979.
Modern library practice ed. by Sheila Ritchie. Elm, 1982.

Chapter Eight

Information sources

Bibliographies

Some of the prime information retrieval tools which librarians use are bibliographies. A bibliography is a list of books. However, not all bibliographies cover the same field or are arranged in the same manner. There are bibliographies which cover one particular subject, while others cover many or all subjects. Some bibliographies are arranged alphabetically and others are classified. Theodore Besterman's *World bibliography of bibliographies* took five volumes to cover its list of bibliographies, and more recently it has been superseded by a number of single volumes on individual subjects, so one can see that the number and range of bibliographies is vast.

British National Bibliography (BNB)

In this country the major bibliography is the *British National Bibliography* which commenced publication in 1950. It is compiled from the legal deposit copies of all new publications/editions which United Kingdom publishers must supply free of charge to the British Library. The bibliography, therefore, claims to be a complete list of all new UK publications. *British National Bibliography* is published weekly and the last copy of each month contains an index covering the entire month. At quarterly intervals, interim cumulations are published which supersede the weekly and monthly parts and there is an annual cumulation in two hardback volumes. The arrangement of the bibliography is like a classified catalogue in printed form.

1   It has a classified sequence in which each book is represented by a full catalogue entry with the Dewey classification number as the heading. The entries are arranged

numerically from the 000s to the 999s in keeping with the Dewey scheme. A typical entry might look like this:

025.52 – Libraries. Reference services

> Grogan, Denis   Practical reference work – London: Bingley, July 1979 – (144)p – (Outlines of modern librarianship).
> ISBN 0-85157-275-8 : £4.50 : CIP entry
> (B79-16309)

The items of information given in the above entry are:
(a) Dewey class number (b) subject, (c) author, (d) title, (e) place of publication, publisher and date, (f) number of pages, (g) series, (h) international standard book number, (i) price, (j) cataloguing in publication information, (k) *BNB* running number.

2   The second sequence in the bibliography is an alphabetical index of authors and titles. The book given as an example above would have the following index entries:

(a) Grogan, Denis   Practical reference work. Bingley. £4.50 CIP entry 025.52 (B79-16309) ISBN 0-85157-275-8

(b) Practical reference work. (Grogan, Denis) Bingley, £4.50 CIP entry 025.52 (B79-16309) ISBN 0-85157-275-8

3   The third sequence in *British National Bibliography* is an alphabetical index of subjects which shows the appropriate Dewey classification number for each subject:

(a) Libraries
    Reference Services 025.52

(b) Reference services. Libraries 025.52

To discover which books have been published on a particular topic, one would consult the subject index to discover the Dewey number and then turn to that number in the classified sequence to find full details of the books. Of course, if either author or title is already known one can turn directly to the author/title index to discover brief details of the book, but for full bibliographical details one would have to turn also to the classified sequence.

British National Bibliography is more or less comprehensive in its coverage of new UK publications/editions but it does not include music or the majority of government publications as these categories are covered by other bibliographies. Reprints are also omitted.

British books in print (BBIP)
The name of this bibliography adequately describes its coverage — namely, a list of all books in print and on sale in the United Kingdom. It therefore includes not only new publications but books published a number of years previously which are still in print. The current printed edition lists 365,660 books from 9805 publishers. The printed edition of *British books in print* is in two hardback volumes published annually and the arrangement is in one straightforward alphabetical sequence of authors, titles and keywords. There is no subject guide to *BBIP* so one must know either the author or the title or a keyword which appears in the title before one can trace further bibliographical details. Examples of entries from *BBIP* are:

1   LIMB, SUE & CORDINGLY, PATRICK Captain Oates: Soldier and Explorer. M8. 176. 77 ill. £12.50 Batsford (11.82) 0 7134 2693 4

The items of information included in the author entry are:
(a) authors
(b) title (including sub-title)
(c) size (ie medium octavo, 176 pages)
(d) number of illustrations
(e) price
(f) publisher
(g) month and year of publication
(h) ISBN

2   Oates, Captain:Soldier and Explorer
(Limb and Cordingly) M8. 176. 77 ill. £12.50 Batsford (11.82) 0 7134 2693 4

Although highly esteemed as a bibliography, *British books in print* had a major drawback in that its publication only once each year meant that it could not remain sufficiently up-to-date. To overcome this, a microfiche edition is now available and this is updated monthly. The arrangement of entries is the same as in the printed edition.

Books in print
This bibliography is the American equivalent of *British books in print*. It is published annually in seven hardback volumes —

two devoted to an author sequence, two to titles and three to the subject guide.

British paperbacks in print

This bibliography of approximately 47,000 paperback books is itself a hardback volume, the 1984 issue being the latest edition. The arrangement is in one alphabetical sequence of authors, titles and subjects which appear as keywords in the titles. For example,

> Lolley, John Louis Your library : what's in it for you? SU R8.160 Ill.
> Self-teaching gdes. sd. £2.75 Wiley (2.74) Bib.

The author entry above gives: (a) author, (b) title with subtitle, (c) size of book and number of pages, (d) illustrated, (e) series, (f) type of binding, (g) price, (h) publisher, (i) month and year of publication, (j) subject.

The book is also listed under its title:

Your library : What's in it for you?

and under the subject keyword:

Library, Your: What's in it for you?;

The bibliographies so far described are general in scope (covering all subjects) but national in extent (covering the publications of one country only). However, there are bibliographies which cover books published in two or more countries.

Books in English

This is a bibliography compiled from the UK MARC records of all new British publications plus LC MARC records of books in the English language added to the stock of the Library of Congress in Washington. *Books in English* also includes cataloguing-in-publication information about forthcoming titles.

The arrangement is alphabetical and the information given includes author, title, edition, publication data, physical description (eg number of pages), series, Library of Congress classification, Dewey classification and ISBN.

Books in English is published on microfiche at bi-monthly intervals, each issue being cumulative, and there is a full annual cumulation. About 100,000 books are covered annually by the bibliography.

The British Library commenced publication of *Books in*

English in 1971 and annual cumulations for the period 1971 to 1980 are still available but these are on ultrafiche only. *Books in English* has now moved to standard microfiche publication. This has made it more useful to most libraries.

Figure 1 Books in English on ultrafiche

Government publications
The British Government, through Her Majesty's Stationery Office and the Publications Division of the Central Office of Information, publishes about 7,000 titles per year. There are more than 90,000 titles at present in print. Government publications include:

1   *Parliamentary publications* (all published by HMSO)
(a) House of Lords publications
    (i) Weekly information bulletin.
    (ii) *Journal of the House of Lords* (1510 to date), published annually.
    (iii) *Official Report of Parliamentary Debates* (Lords' *Hansard*).
    (iv) Papers and Bills.

(b) House of Commons publications
  (i) Weekly information bulletin.
 (ii) *Journal of the House of Commons*, published annually. Each volume has its own index. A general (cumulative) index is published every ten years.
(iii) Official *Report* of Parliamentary Debates (Commons' *Hansard*).
 (iv) Bills.
  (v) Papers.

The journals listed above are large and expensive so few public libraries stock them.

Hansard is published daily (printed overnight). It is often described as a 'verbatim report' but in fact it is discreetly edited. However, it is accurate and completely unbiased. The 'Commons'' *Hansard* and the 'Lords'' *Hansard* are separate.

There is a *Weekly Hansard* and separate weekly index, plus bound volumes (of uniform physical size so the number of the parts included varies) accompanied by an index. A consolidated sessional index is also published. The indexes include entries under subjects and under MPs' names.

(c) Commons' papers and Lords' papers. These are numbered serially each session, eg
  HC 298, 1969-70
  HL 78, 1969-70

(d) Command papers. That is, papers presented to Parliament by a minister on his own initiative (in theory, they are presented by *command* of Her Majesty).
  Command papers also include:
  Foreign and Commonwealth Office papers.
  White papers, ie statements on government policy.
  Statistical reports, etc.
  Command papers are numbered in series. We are now in the fifth series (1956 onwards).

(e) Bills, Acts and measures. Bills are printed on pale green paper, and numbered serially within each session (in brackets if it is a Commons Bill, in parentheses if a Lords Bill).
  Public General Acts are public Bills which have been

passed by both Houses and given royal assent. They are first published separately then in bound annual volumes (appearing every March), including indexes.

There are also tables and indexes to local and personal Acts (Acts arising from private members' Bills).

Church Assembly Measures are those passed by the National Assembly of the Church of England and given royal assent.

2 *Non-Parliamentary publications*
These include:

(a) *Statutory instruments.* That is, regulations made by a minister under the authority of an Act of Parliament (delegated legislation). They are first published singly, numbered serially within each year, then in annual bound volumes.

(b) *Reports.* For example, *Registrar General's statistical review of England and Wales; Traffic in towns* (Buchanan report); *The reshaping of British Railways* (Beeching report).

3 *Periodicals*

(a) *London Gazette.* Published four times each week, with occasional special supplements, and with a quarterly index, it contains a comprehensive range of official information. (Called the *Oxford Gasette* from 1665 until 1910 when it changed its name to the *London Gazette.*)

(b) *Monthly Digest of Statistics.* Detailed statistics on a wide range of subjects.

Obviously, librarians require the assistance of catalogues, guides and indexes to help them to find their way through such an array of government publications. Fortunately HMSO publishes quite a number of helpful guides and these include:

1 *Daily List*
Published Monday to Friday, excluding Bank holidays.
Contents:
(a) Parliamentary publications arranged by series.
(b) Non-Parliamentary publications arranged alphabetically by department.

(c) Reprints with altered prices/codes.
(d) Publications sold but not published by HMSO.
(e) Corrections to previous *Daily Lists.*
(f) List of Statutory Instruments issued.
Information given: Author (corporate or personal), title, series, ISBN, number of pages, price, size.

2 *Monthly Catalogue*
Monthly cumulation of *Daily Lists.* Contents:
(a) Parliamentary publications, arranged by series.
(b) Classified list (i) Non-Parliamentary (ii) Parliamentary, arranged alphabetically by department.
(c) Index.
(d) Index of ISBN.
(Statutory instruments are excluded.)
(Note: Parliamentary publications are listed twice, ie under series and under department.)

3 *Monthly Select List*
Distributed as a folder with the *Monthly Catalogue.* It is a short annotated bibliography of some publications which are likely to be of wide interest.

4 *Annual Catalogue*
A cumulation of the *Monthly Catalogue,* appearing four to five months following the end of the year covered. Excludes Statutory Instruments and publications of international organizations for which HMSO is agent. Arrangement is the same as the *Monthly Catalogue.*

5 *Consolidated index*
to government publications – published every five years since 1936.

6 *Sectional lists*
These are lists of all the publications in print (and sometimes out of print) of individual departments, eg Department of Education and Science, or on special topics, eg Building; Royal Commissions 1937-70. About 40 lists are available, free of charge.

7 *Card index catalogue service*
Librarians may purchase pre-printed catalogue cards for HMSO publications.

8   *Weekly local government list*
    A weekly list of government publications from HMSO:
    a selection of interest to local authorities. Arrangement is
    under broad subject headings, eg education, housing,
    planning, public health, etc.

9   *List of statutory instruments*
    Monthly with annual cumulations. Arranged alphabeti-
    cally by subject, with index of SI numbers, index of
    ISBNs and an alphabetical subject index. The subject
    index cumulates each month.

Specialist bibliographies
Almost every subject field has its own specialist bibliography
or bibliographies. Some are large and scholarly works while
some are designed as simple guides to source material for the
student or the man in the street wishing to read up on a
particular topic.

British Catalogue of Music
The catalogue covers music sheets and scores and books
about music which have been recently published in Britain.
As with *British National Bibliography*, the *British Catalogue
of Music* is compiled from legal deposit copies received by
the Copyright Receipt Office of the British Library. It is
published quarterly with an annual cumulation, and is
arranged in two separate sequences:
1   a classified sequence arranged by the Coates faceted
    classification scheme;
2   an alphabetical index of titles, composers, arrangers, etc.
The coverage is comprehensive apart from some types of pop
music and modern dance music.

British Catalogue of Audiovisual Materials
This catalogue, published by British Library Bibliographic
Services Division, is based on the stock of the Inner London
Education Authority's Centre for Learning Resources. In
addition, information is gleaned from publishers and from
the British Universities Film Council.
    The catalogue is arranged in three sequences:
1   classified sequence arranged by Dewey numbers;
2   an alphabetical index of titles, series, and originators;

3   an alphabetical subject index which gives the relevant Dewey number for each subject.

The arrangement and method of consultation is therefore identical to *British National Bibliography* but the information in the main entries differs from *BNB* because of the nature of the non-book media. Sample of an entry from the classified sequence:

> 027.625   —   Children's libraries. Guidance for users.
> The junior library. — London, Slide Centre, 1967.
> 3p; 33cm
> 24 slides : col.
> (293-4)
> Leaflet contains teacher's notes.

The information in the above entry includes (a) Dewey classification number, (b) subject, (c) title, (d) place of publication, publisher and date, (e) number of pages (in the accompanying leaflet) and its shelf height, (f) number of slides in the set and the fact that they are coloured, (g) annotation or further notes about the item.

The catalogue covers filmstrips, slides, films, filmloops, portfolios, posters, charts, overhead projection transparencies, kits, cassettes, gramophone records, work cards, educational games, spirit masters, etc, but excludes videorecordings and most 16mm films which are already listed in the *British National Film Catalogue*, and also musical sound recordings.

A supplement to the main catalogue was published in 1981.

British National Film Catalogue

Listed in this catalogue are British and foreign films which have recently been made available in this country. It commenced publication in 1963 and appears quarterly with an annual cumulation. The arrangement is in two main sequences:

1   non-fiction films arranged in classified order by the Universal Decimal Classification scheme;
2   fiction films arranged alphabetically by title.

There are also indexes of subjects, titles, distributors, etc. The information about each film includes the producer and distributor, running time, whether sound or silent, black and white or colour. Feature films and newsreels are excluded from the catalogue's coverage as they are dealt with in the *Monthly Film Bulletin.*

As has been stated previously, practically every field of knowledge has its own specialist bibliographies and they are far too numerous to list. It may suffice to name just a few examples:

1   Burrington, G A *How to find out about the social sciences.* Oxford, Pergamon, 1975.
2   Blackstone, T *Social policy and administration in Britain: a bibliography.* Pinter, 1975.
3   Vernon, K D C *Use of management and business literature.* London, Butterworths, 1975.
4   Dove, Jack *Fine arts* (Reader's Guide series). London, Bingley, 1966.

Indexes to periodicals

Periodicals are important as information sources because they are published more frequently than books and are therefore more up-to-date. However, it would be a time consuming task for the student or researcher to sit down with piles of periodicals, frantically scanning contents lists to try to trace articles on his chosen topic. Fortunately, he does not have to do the spadework as, in most cases, it has already been done and published indexes provide a short cut to discovering what has appeared in periodicals. Again, there are too many indexes to list them all so it must suffice to consider a few of the better known ones.

British Humanities Index

The index appears in paperback format at quarterly intervals but there is also a bound annual cumulation. The 369 periodicals which are scanned include *History Today, Geographical Magazine, The Economist, Music Review, Listener, New Statesman, New Society* and *The Guardian, The Times* and *The Sunday Times.* The index itself is an alphabetical list of subjects with related headings and 'see' references, and the annual volume includes an author index also. The information given about an article is as follows:

Libraries, National : England : British Library
    Preserving the world's memory. Keith Spence.
    Country Life, 173 (21 Apr 83) p1012-13. il.

ie Subject heading
    Title. Author. Name of periodical.
    Issue number. Date. Page numbers.

If the article is illustrated the abbreviation 'il.' is given and if it includes a bibliography the abbreviation 'refs' appears.

British Education Index
The British Library publishes this index in quarterly paperback issues with a bound annual cumulation. Over 300 educational journals are scanned, and the arrangement of the index is as follows:

1 List of periodicals indexed, arranged alphabetically.
2 Subject list of articles. The arrangement of this sequence is alphabetical by subject and the information included is demonstrated in the example given below:
   LIBRARIES. Polytechnics
     Use by students
       Student information needs/E Blackie and J M Smith. — Bull. Educ. Res., Nos. 23/24; Summer 82. — p.3-9

   ie (a) broad subject heading, (b) specific subject, (c) title, (d) authors, (e) name of periodical (*Bulletin of Educational Research*), (f) volume and/or part number, (g) date, (h) page numbers.
3 Author index. In this sequence our example is listed under Blackie and under Smith and the items of information from (c)–(h) above are given again.

Current Technology Index (previously known as *British Technology Index*)
Because of the need to be really up-to-date in the field of technology, this index is published monthly but also has an annual bound cumulation. Its subject coverage spans all branches of engineering, along with chemical technology and manufacturing. The index is arranged in two sequences:

1 alphabetical subject index which gives details of titles of articles, authors and sources;
2 author index which quotes the source of the article and also gives the first word or phrase of the subject heading under which it is listed in the main sequence.

Applied Science and Technology Index
The three indexes discussed so far have all been British publications, but there are many foreign indexes, some of which are international in coverage. One such index is the *Applied Science and Technology Index*. It is published in the USA

but covers 307 English language periodicals regardless of their country of origin. The index appears monthly, except July, in paperback format with a bound annual cumulation. The arrangement is alphabetical by subject but there is an additional brief list of book reviews arranged by author.

Indexes to indexes
The range of indexes to periodicals is so vast that there are even indexes to indexes such as:

> Harzfield, L A *Periodical indexes in the social sciences and humanities: a subject guide.* Scarecrow Press, 1978.

Citation indexes
A citation index is 'an ordered list of references (cited works) in which each reference is followed by a list of the sources (citing works) which cite it'. In other words, if a person doing research in a particular field knows of one book which is useful to him he can then trace other authors who have referred to that book in their published work. Their books will consequently be of use to the researcher as they are bound to cover the same subject area. The two prime examples of this kind of reference tool are *Science Citation Index* and *Social Sciences Citation Index*.

Abstracts
Indexes to periodicals are extremely useful tools for discovering which articles have been published on a given topic but they give only subject headings and titles of articles as clues to their content. An abstracting service, on the other hand, gives a précis of each article so it provides a much more informative guide. Most subject areas are covered by abstracting services and the following are examples.

Library and Information Sciences Abstracts (LISA)
LISA is published monthly by The Library Association. The abstracts are arranged in classified order using a classification scheme devised by the Classification Research Group which utilizes upper and lower case letters and numerals in its notation. Each abstract is also identified by a running number. For example,

HykGpAw23—*Relationship with* Teachers   83/3740
    Grasping nettles, smoking marijuana or working with the enemy. Richard Owen. *Review*, 10(2) June 82, 9-11. illus. 11 refs.
    Examination of the relationship between the school librarian and teacher, advocating closer liaison between the 2, to motivate students to use the library and its resources. (D.A.C.)

The example shown above has been selected because of the brief, concise, yet informative abstract, but most abstracts are considerably longer and more detailed.

Each issue of *LISA* contains a subject index and an author index which link with the classified list by means of the abstract number. The indexes are easily identifiable because they are printed on coloured paper. The entries in these indexes for the example shown are:

1   Subject index

School libraries   **School teachers**
    3737–3743   *See* Teachers
Teachers
    Lecturers *See* Lecturers
    Relationship with School
    libraries 3740

2   Author index
    Owen, Richard 3740

In addition to each issue's indexes there are also annual and five-yearly cumulated indexes.

Children's Literature Abstracts
The Children's Libraries Section of the International Federation of Library Associations publishes *Children's Literature Abstracts* at quarterly intervals. The coverage includes children's reading, children's books, their authors and illustrators, book selection and children's literature awards. It is international in scope but selective in content. The abstracts are arranged in broad subject categories and identified by a running number. The March issue each year contains an author index and a subject index to the previous year's issues.

Compilation of booklists and bulletins

Most libraries produce their own booklists and bulletins from time to time. These are usually offered free of charge to library members as part of the library's promotional services. The bibliographies may be lists of recent additions to stock, works by a particular author, fiction of a particular type or non-fiction covering a specific subject. Bibliographies are sometimes produced to accompany exhibitions and displays, or to relate to extra-library activities such as children's story hours, film shows or outings, or for special events such as National Library Week.

The home-produced bibliographies will normally relate to a library's own stock and will be compiled from information gleaned from the library's catalogue. Sometimes, the bibliographies are straightforward lists of authors and titles but they may also be annotated to include a short summary or appraisal of each book. Printing costs are high so libraries often produce their own booklists and bulletins using offset-litho or absorption duplication (Roneo, Gestetner, etc) machines. A few libraries also employ staff trained at art college so that the artwork, lettering and general standard of production of all publicity and display materials is high.

Special libraries, particularly academic and industrial libraries, will circulate home-produced bulletins to their own clientele in an effort to keep them up-to-date in their own field of expertise. Abstracts bulletins supplement pub-

Figure 2 A home produced bibliography

lished abstracts and have the advantages of being more up-to-date and based on the individual library's own holdings. They can also cover internal reports and foreign language materials which would not be encompassed by published abstracts. It must be appreciated, however, that a great deal of staff time is taken up in reading, summarizing and evaluating books and periodical articles if an abstracts bulletin is to be produced.

A simpler method, though less informative is to produce a titles bulletin whereby only the titles, authors and sources of periodical articles and books are given. The titles are usually grouped under subject headings so that the reader does not have to peruse the entire list to find the items relevant to his subject field.

One popular form of current awareness service involves the photocopying of the contents lists of specified periodicals. The photocopies are then sent to particular individuals who require to be kept informed about current literature in their specialist field.

Libraries with ready access to a computer can produce print-outs of titles or abstracts and operate a service known as SDI or selective dissemination of information.

Reference books
The number and range of reference books is vast and years of study and practice are necessary before one can acquire the knowledge and expertise which reference librarians demonstrate. Nevertheless, library assistants and, indeed, library users will find it useful to have some knowledge of reference books and their coverage. There are many types and formats of reference books and these include dictionaries, encyclopaedias, directories, yearbooks and so on.

Dictionaries
Dictionaries can be divided into the following types:
1 *Language dictionaries*
  (a) National, ie the language of a particular country or countries. These can be English or foreign. National dictionaries can be subdivided into two types:
      (i) Etymological, ie showing the origin of words and tracing the development of meaning over the years, eg *Oxford English dictionary*, 13 volumes plus 3 supplements.

(ii) Current, ie giving only the present-day meaning of words, eg *Concise Oxford dictionary of current English.*

(b) Bilingual, ie dictionaries which list the words of one language but give the meaning or synonyms in another language, eg *Cassell's Spanish-English English-Spanish dictionary; Oxford-Harrap Standard German—English dictionary*, 3 volumes.

2   *Specialist dictionaries*, which list only those terms which pertain to a particular subject (like an extended glossary). Instead of just giving synonyms, some give considerable information about each specific topic and so are more like encyclopaedias than dictionaries, eg *Black's Bible dictionary* and the *New Grove dictionary of music and musicians*, 20 volumes. Under the heading of specialist dictionaries one can also include:

dictionaries of synonyms,
dictionaries of grammar and usage,
dictionaries of abbreviations,
dictionaries of prosody, ie rhyming dictionaries,
dictionaries of Christian (personal) names.

3   *Biographical dictionaries.* These are of three kinds:

(a) International and general, eg *Webster's biographical dictionary* (includes living and deceased persons) and *The international who's who* (living persons only).

(b) National and general, which can be subdivided into two kinds:

(i) Current — including only living persons, eg *Who's who.*

(ii) Retrospective — including only deceased persons, eg *Dictionary of national biography*, and *Who was who.*

(c) Specialist, which cover persons concerned with particular professions, defined areas of knowledge or specified strata of society, eg

(i) *Burke's royal families of the world.*

(ii) *Who's who in broadcasting.*

(iii) *Who's who in the arts and literature.*

Encyclopaedias

An encyclopaedia is a quick reference tool providing information on (1) every branch of knowledge (general) or (2) one field of knowledge (specialist).

The arrangement is usually alphabetical under subject headings which may be broad or specific. However, some encyclopaedias group topics together under very broad subject areas, eg the *Oxford junior encyclopaedia* which groups subjects under such broad heads as 'The arts', 'Engineering', etc devoting one complete volume to each broad grouping.

The more scholarly encyclopaedias usually have lengthy articles written by subject specialists, and the articles are often signed (or initialled) by the writer. Popular encyclopaedias tend towards short articles on specific topics and these are not signed.

Most multi-volume encyclopaedias include an index (sometimes a separate index volume) which lists subjects alphabetically and gives the volume and page number where information can be found. The index usually has 'see also' references.

Illustrations, plates, maps, etc form a vital part of an encyclopaedia and should not be separated from the text to which they refer.

A select list of encyclopaedias:

General — one volume
1   *Hutchinson's new twentieth century encyclopaedia*
2   *Pears cyclopaedia*

General — multi-volume
1   *Encyclopedia Americana*
2   *Encyclopaedia Britannica*
3   *Everyman's encyclopaedia*

General — for young people
1   *Black's children's encyclopedia*
2   *Children's Britannica*
3   *Oxford junior encyclopaedia*
4   *World book encyclopedia*

Specialist
1   *Careers encyclopaedia*
2   *Hastings' encyclopaedia of religion and ethics*
3   *McGraw-Hill encyclopedia of science and technology*
4   *Van Nostrand's scientific encyclopedia*

Directories
A directory is a list of persons, organizations, professions, industries or trades. The list is systematically arranged, either in alphabetical or in classified order. Because the information in directories becomes out-of-date fairly rapidly they are either published annually or new editions are brought out every two or three years.

Types of directory:

1 *Local directories* — usually for the larger towns and cities only. These normally include
   (a) a list of private residents, arranged alphabetically by surname;
   (b) an alphabetical list of streets, giving the name of the occupier of each property in each street;
   (c) a classified list of trades — similar to the 'yellow pages' in a telephone directory;
   (d) lists of establishments such as places of worship, places of entertainment, etc, eg *Kelly's Post Office London directory.*

2 *Professional directories* — these are lists of qualified practitioners in particular professions, and include brief biographical details, and sometimes information about the profession itself. For example,
   (a) *Directory of directors.*
   (b) *Law list* — annual;
   (c) *Library Association yearbook* — annual;
   (d) *Medical directory* — annual.

3 *Trade directories*
   (a) General and national — ie all the trades and industries of a particular country. Arrangement is usually classified, or alphabetical, by the type of trade or industry, with an additional alphabetical list of individual firms, eg *Kelly's manufacturers and merchants directory; Kompass.*
   (b) Specialist and national — ie concerned with one field of industry in a particular country, eg *British plastics yearbook.*

4 *Telephone directories* — each telephone directory covers the subscribers in a defined geographical area. The main list is alphabetical by name of subscriber but the 'yellow

pages' section which is separately published contains a classified list of subscribers arranged by type of industry or service. Most are now available in microfiche.

Yearbooks

A yearbook is a reference book which is published annually, and the word 'yearbook' is sometimes incorporated in the title. Yearbooks usually give up-to-date statistical information and may also include a review of the events of the previous year, eg *Statesman's yearbook.*

Almanacs

An almanac, sometimes spelt 'almanack', was originally an annual publication which gave astronomical information such as times of sunrise and sunset, the moon's phases, etc but allied this to astrological predictions of the events of the coming year. The predictive element has now disappeared from the major almanacs but the astronomical information has been retained. *Whitaker's almanack* is the best known example and it contains a wealth of information about the governments, education systems, products, imports and exports, etc of all the countries of the world. An example of an almanac which is concerned less with statistical information and world events and more about tide tables and so on is the *Nautical almanac.*

Concordances

A concordance is an alphabetical list of all the important subjects, persons, places which have been named in a particular work. It does not give any descriptive information about them but gives the context of each word and the source, eg
1   *Cruden's complete concordance to the Old and New Testaments;*
2   *Concordance to the poetical and dramatic works of Alfred Lord Tennyson* (Baker, A E).

Maps and atlases

A map is a representation, usually flat, of the whole or a part of the earth's surface or of the celestial sphere. An atlas is a collection of maps bound together. The world 'atlas' was first used in this sense by Mercator from the figure of the mythological Atlas which was often used as the frontispiece of early collections of maps. It has come to mean any volume containing not only maps, but also plates, engravings, charts and tables, with or without descriptive text. It is sometimes used as the name of a volume in which subjects are presented in tabular form.

While it is generally recognized that atlases are essential in studying history, geography and other branches of social sciences, it is becoming increasingly apparent that many atlases are valuable also as general reference books because of the descriptive materials they contain in addition to maps. Today, maps are necessary companions to the daily newspaper and radio and television news commentary, verifying names, places and events in the news and presenting them in proper geographical relationship to other names, places and events.

There are many sources of maps. Most of the general encyclopaedias include maps either in a separate volume or as illustrative material within the text; encyclopaedia yearbooks include up-to-date maps; many handbooks, almanacs, newspapers and periodicals also contain maps. However, the atlas is the reference book designed primarily to provide maps.

Atlases vary in quality and they vary in coverage according to the country of publication. In addition to topographical information they may also show administrative boundaries, the distribution of industries or population, the extent of settlement at a particular period, or the use to which land is put.

Evaluating an atlas
1   The scope
    (a) Is it worldwide in coverage, or is it limited to one or more regions?
    (b) Does it include all kinds of maps, or only maps of a specific nature?
    (c) Does it provide descriptive material about the various geographical locations?
2   The place of publication as an indication of emphasis.
3   The date of publication as an indication of its up-to-dateness.
4   The index.

(a) Is there one comprehensive index for the entire atlas, or are there separate indexes for each volume or section?

(b) Is the index a separate volume, or is it a part of the atlas?

(c) Does it indicate pronunciation?

(d) Is the reference to the location on a given map clear and definite?

5 The quality and content of the maps.

(a) Is the scale indicated clearly?

(b) Are the symbols distinct and easily read?

(c) Are the projections in keeping with the purpose of the map?

(d) Is the lettering clear and legible?

(e) Is the colouring varied and well differentiated?

(f) Are the names of countries given in the language of each country or in translation?

Explanation of terms

1 Scale — the distance as shown on the map in relation to actual distance. This is given as a ratio, eg 1:50 000.

2 Projection — the way in which the curved surface of the earth is portrayed on the flat surface of the map.

3 Elevation — the height of the earth's surface above sea level. This can be shown by colour, by countour lines, etc.

4 Reference system — the method by which one can locate a place on a map, eg

(a) degrees of latitude and longitude;

(b) a grid reference.

Gazetteers

A gazetteer is a dictionary of geographical places. In addition to geographical location, it gives historical, statistical, cultural and other relevant information about these places. It may also indicate pronunciation. Because they provide a variety of factual material about places, gazetteers are important reference sources. Recent editions describe a place as it is now; old editions give historical information about it. The economic growth or decline of a town or city, as indicated by data on population, types of industries, schools and so on, will often be shown by the brief facts given in gazetteers over a period of years. Some gazetteers include entries for rivers, capes and other geographical features.

In using a gazetteer, it is important to note the publication date as an indication of the recency of the material; the system of pronunciation and the abbreviations used; the arrangement of the material; and any additional material, such as maps and tables, which may be included in appendices.

Reference works of unusual format

Some reference works are not published as bound volumes but in separately produced parts. One such work is *Keesing's contemporary archives* which is an authoritative source of information on current events throughout the world. To ensure that the information is up-to-date, printed pages are posted to subscribers at weekly intervals and these must be inserted into the loose-leaf binders provided. Indexes of subjects and of names are similarly supplied at regular intervals with accompanying instructions about the discarding of superseded indexes.

The *Barbour index* builds up in a similar fashion in its many loose-leaf binders, but a library's subscription covers the service of an employee of the *Barbour index* who will come along to do the insertions and withdrawals on one's behalf. The index is classified by the construction industry's Sfb classification scheme and its coverage is of products, building plans and designs and other topics related to the construction industry.

Another format of reference work is that of printed cards or slips which have to be filed in filing cabinet drawers, and again new items have to be inserted and old ones discarded to ensure currency of information. One such service is that of Extel Statistical Services which covers current information about industrial firms, including company profits and share prices.

Microfilm and microfiche formats are now commonplace in most libraries. Several bibliographies, indexes and abstracts are available in microform editions and one can usually purchase complete back runs as well as the current issues. One example of a reference source in microform is Acomplis Index produced by the Greater London Council. It is an alphabetical subject index to books and periodical articles covering many subject fields and updated at quarterly intervals. It is produced in cassetted microfilm. British Standards are also available in cassetted microfilm format.

Modern technology has introduced into libraries the concept of instant information. Two main systems are available to libraries. The first is Teletext, an information service accessed via a television set with teletext facilities. The second is Viewdata, a Post Office system.

Teletext
A BBC engineer working on the transmission of programmes with subtitles for the deaf saw the possibility of developing the technique into an information service which viewers could access as required during normal transmission times. The cost of the Teletext service is borne out of normal revenue from TV licences and advertising so the user does not pay directly for the information provided. However, it is necessary to have a TV set which incorporates Teletext facilities.

Transmission began on BBC 1 in September 1974, but all four channels now have a teletext service. BBC 1 and BBC 2 use the name CEEFAX which is just a variant of the words 'see facts'. ITV's channels 3 and 4 operate their teletext service under the acronym ORACLE, which stands for Optical Reception of Announcements by Coded Line Electronics.

To access information a remote control handset is used. First, the required channel is selected by pressing the appropriate key and then pressing the button marked 'text'. Pages of text then appear in a pre-determined sequence so the user has to key in the number of the page he requires. Index pages are provided so normally the user will initially key in the number of the main index page in order to discover the page numbers of the required subject area, whether it is sports results, the latest news, weather or road reports or cookery recipes. There can be a delay of several seconds before the chosen page appears on the screen. A useful addition to the service is the provision of a 24-hour clock at the top of each page. This provides a cheaper and quicker method of getting an accurate time check than telephoning the 'speaking clock'.

The disadvantages of Ceefax are:
1 The service can be used only during normal TV transmission times.
2 The viewer can access information only if the provider has included it. Ceefax and Oracle cover topics of general interest only.

3   The time lapse before the required page appears can be-
    come irritating.
4   There is no two-way communication.

Viewdata
The British Post Office system, Prestel, began in September
1979. The user requires a television set or visual display unit
which is connected via the telephone network to the Prestel
computer, and also a keypad or keyboard for calling up the
required information.

   As there is a charge for the Prestel service the user is
required to have a customer identification number. The
number gives British Telecom access to the user's name and
address so that regular accounts can be sent to users in much
the same way as telephone bills. The cost to the user covers
the telephone charge which is based in the normal way on
units (ie amount of time connected and rate of unit depending on day and time). In addition, the user pays for the
connection to the computer and also for certain pages of
information which may be accessed. Some pages are free but
others bear a charge which is set by the information provider.
The cost appears at the top of the screen so that the user can
keep a tally of the bill he will have to pay. Up-to-the minute
information about fluctuations in the money market is
probably the most expensive to access.

   The recovering of costs from the individual Prestel user
may present a problem to libraries so some precautionary
measures may be taken. These include the use of a personal
password in addition to the user identification number to
prevent unauthorized use of the system and also the payment
of a deposit by the user to ensure he or she doesn't slip out
of the library undetected without paying for the information
pages accessed.

   A typical procedure would be as follows:
1   Payment of deposit by user.
2   Log on by depressing the appropriate keys on the keypad
    or keyboard.
3   Key in the user identification number.
4   Telephone the computer's number and make connection.
5   Key in the personal password.
Note: Steps 2 to 5 would be carried out by library staff and
not by the user. This would ensure the user identification

number, computer phone number and password are not disclosed.

Instructions covering some steps of the procedure are flashed up on the screen.

6 Press the appropriate key to call up the 'menu' page ie the index.

7 Press the required number for the information category required to access a more specific index.

8 Key in the page number.

9 When all the required information has been accessed, depress the appropriate key to call up the total charge incurred for pages.

10 Log off and disconnect.

The user's Prestel equipment can be linked with a mini-computer such as a BBC micro. Information can then be downloaded on to a floppy disc and stored for subsequent use.

Additional features of Prestel include

1 *Mailbox.* Messages can be sent by one Prestel user and received by any other Prestel user.

2 *Closed user groups.* Some information providers do not want certain information to be available to all. Those for whom the information is intended are given a special password.

3 *Gateway.* Other computers eg those belonging to large industrial firms can be connected to the Prestel network. This enables certain categories of user to access information from these private computers with the owner's agreement.

The advantages of Viewdata are:

1 Two-way communication.

2 Wider range of information available.

3 Business information is very up-to-date.

4 Pages appear instantaneously. There is no pre-determined order of storage and retrieval.

5 Possibility of downloading and storing information.

6 Extra facilities available, eg Mailbox.

7 Libraries can order free material such as travel brochures on Prestel.

The disadvantages of Viewdata are:

1 The costs incurred (capital expenditure on equipment, telephone charges, page charges).

2   All telephone lines to the computer may be engaged at peak periods.
3   The problems associated with charging the individual user for the service.
4   Some information providers do not update their data with sufficient frequency.

On-line computer information retrieval systems offer equally rapid access to data banks and most large libraries now offer this service. The purpose differs from that of Teletext and Viewdata in that on-line information retrieval is mainly used for rapid access to bibliographical data, ie to trace details of books and/or periodical articles.

Many systems are available to libraries, Dialog and Blaise-line probably being the most commonly used.

1   *DIALOG (Lockheed Information Systems)*
    The Dialog system covers the fields of:

    agriculture and nutrition (6 databases);
    bibliography — books and monographs (7 databases);
    business/economics, including management (52 databases);
    chemistry (13 databases);
    current affairs (13 databases);
    directories (8 databases);
    education (6 databases);
    energy and environment (16 databases);
    foundations and grants (4 databases);
    law and government (16 databases);
    materials sciences (12 databases);
    medicine and biosciences (18 databases);
    multidisciplinary (eg dissertation abstracts) (4 databases);
    online training and practice (tapping 14 databases);
    patents and trademarks (9 databases);
    science and technology (20 databases);
    social sciences and humanities (19 databases).

    Most of Dialog's databases are American but some important British sources can be accessed, eg INSPEC (Institution of Electrical Engineers) and LISA (Library and Information Science Abstracts).

2   *BLAISE-LINE (British Library Automated Information Service on line)*
    Blaise-line includes:

(a) The MARC files — ie UK MARC which gives bibliographical details of British publications, LC MARC which covers American books and AV MARC which provides information on audio visual aids.

(b) British Education Index, the major index to British educational periodicals.

(c) Conference proceedings index.

(d) ESTC (Eighteenth Century Short Title Catalogue)

(e) HELPIS (Audio visual aids designed for use in colleges and universities)

Blaise-line is particularly useful to library staff as on trace or check Dewey classification numbers, ISBN's and other bibliographical details.

The usual procedure for accessing information from on-line computer networks is as follows:

1 Switch on the equipment. Normally a cursor appears on the VDU screen to indicate that the equipment is powered.

2 Move the switch to either half or full duplex, whichever is required.

3 Telephone the number of the selected system, eg Dialog, Blaise, etc.

4 Attach the telephone handset to the acoustic data coupler as soon as the high pitched tone is heard.

5 Enter the library's password. Normally the command 'enter password' appears on the VDU screen and must be acted upon before one can continue the search.

6 Call up the required file. Each file is identified by a number which can be traced in the user manual. In some systems, the command is acceptable as a word, eg 'begin', or a letter, eg 'b', or a symbol, eg '!', followed by the number of the file.

7 The topic on which you are seeking information must be expressed as a term or string of terms which most aptly describe the subject. A library may have a published thesaurus of acceptable terms to assist in the task of selection. When a term is sought (preceded by the command 'Select', 'S' or '#') the computer searches its memory and then replies with the number of references to that term which are in the selected file. To narrow the search, one will ask the computer to search for a second or third term which will modify the first one sought and

then combine these by using the command 'combine' 'c' or '#'.

8 One can then choose to have brief or full details of some or all of the fruits of the search and these can be typed on-line, ie the results appear there and then not only on the VDU screen but also on a roll of paper which spills

Figure 3 Prestel Micronet (in use in the library of the Chelmer Institute, Chelmsford)

out of the attached printer at a rate of knots. Alternatively one can use the command 'print' instead of 'type' and one will then receive the information by post within a few days.

9 On completion of the search, the VDU will flash up details of the costs accrued for which the library will later be billed. After logging off, the telephone handset is replaced and the equipment switched off.

Basic reference books

Time and space do not allow the inclusion of a comprehensive list and survey of all available reference works. However, the following is a list of basic reference books broadly grouped by Dewey's ten main classes.

1   General knowledge and librarianship
   Aslib directory
   Collins' dictionary of abbreviations
   Guinness book of records
   One volume encyclopaedia:
   Pears cyclopaedia
   Multi-volume encyclopaedias:
   Encyclopedia Americana
   Encyclopaedia Britannica
   Everyman's encyclopaedia
   Encyclopaedias for children:
   Black's children's encyclopaedia
   Children's Britannica
   Oxford junior encyclopaedia
   World book encyclopedia

1(a) Newspapers and periodicals:
   Abstracts, indexes, directories, etc.
   Abstracts:
   Children's literature abstracts
   Library and information science abstracts
   RICS abstracts
   Indexes:
   British education index
   British humanities index
   Current technology index
   Times index

Directories and guides:
Ulrich's international periodicals directory
Willing's press guide
Catalogues of library holdings:
British union catalogue of periodicals
Essex union list of serials (on microfiche)

2   *Religion*
    Black's Bible dictionary
    Cruden's complete concordance to the Old and New Testaments
    Hastings' encyclopaedia of religion and ethics
    Oxford Bible atlas
    Oxford dictionary of the Christian church

3   *Social sciences*
    Directory of directors
    Dod's parliamentary companion
    Hansard
    Municipal yearbook
    Statesman's yearbook
    Titles and forms of address
    Whitaker's almanack
    Education:
    Careers encyclopedia
    Educational authorities directory and annual
    Public and preparatory schools year book
    University calendars and handbooks
    World of learning
    Post Office:
    Post Office guide
    Telephone directories

4   *Languages*
    See the section on dictionaries, pp147-8.

5   *Science and technology*
&   *Black's medical dictionary*
6   *British Standards yearbook*
    Jane's all the world's aircraft
    Jane's fighting ships
    Kelly's manufacturers and merchants directory

Kempe's engineers yearbook
Kompass United Kingdom
McGraw-Hill encyclopedia of science and technology
Machinery's handbook
Medical register
Van Nostrand's scientific encyclopedia

7   *The arts*

Encyclopaedia of world art
Grove's dictionary of music and musicians
Kobbe's complete opera book
Official rules of sports and games
Oxford companion to music
Oxford companion to the theatre
Phoenix dictionary of games
Who's who in the arts and literature
Wisden's cricketers' almanack

8   *Literature*

Brewer's dictionary of phrase and fable
Fiction index and junior fiction index
International encyclopaedia of quotations
Oxford companion to classical literature
Oxford companion to English literature
Oxford dictionary of quotations
Sequels, v.1: Adult books, v.2: Junior books
Writers' and artists' yearbook

9   *History*

Annual register of world events
Britain: an official handbook
Chambers' dictionary of dates
Encyclopaedia of world history
Keesing's contemporary archives
Muir's historical atlas, ancient, medieval and modern
Victoria history of the counties of England

9(a) *Geography*

Bartholomew's gazetteer of Britain
Ordnance survey maps
Times atlas of the world

9(b) Biography

>*Burke's royal families of the world*
>*Chambers' biographical dictionary*
>*Dictionary of national biography*
>*International who's who*
>*Webster's biographical dictionary*
>*Who's who*
>*Who was who*

10 Local information

>*Kelly's directory* of the locality
>*Ordnance survey map(s)* of the locality
>*Telephone directory* of the locality

Audio-visual materials and equipment
Libraries have always been repositories of knowledge in whatever formats were available. Thus, libraries of ancient times stored clay tablets, papyrus rolls, parchment scrolls and so on. As they have become readily available, libraries have also kept newspaper cuttings, charts, maps, mounted illustrations and photographs. In recent years, the range and diversity of formats has increased dramatically and public libraries stock and offer for loan slides, filmstrips, gramophone records, tapes, cassettes, and, in some instances, framed works of art.

Academic libraries house an even wider range of audio-visual media to meet the needs of pupils, students and staff. Their stocks may include films, filmloops, overhead projection transparencies, wallcharts, videotapes/cassettes, models, kits, workcards, handouts, educational games, nature specimens, artefacts and realia (eg fossils).

It is unfortunate that some institutions separate the printed materials from the non-print media and maintain a library and a resource centre as two separate entities under completely different management. This is not a sensible arrangement as the person seeking information normally wants it and happily accepts it in whatever format is available. In fact a variety of formats is often more helpful than a single format. For example, the child doing a project about birds will require books to give him background information, a record or cassette to let him hear bird-song, and a film to help him to appreciate bird flight. How much easier it would be for that pupil if all the various media were listed together in the catalogue and housed together in one area.

Non-print media are extremely useful sources of information but, despite Marshall McLuhan's predictions of several years ago, the book has not yet been ousted. It must be remembered that books are still the most important resources for leaning.

Multi-media items are often more susceptible to damage than books and their varied shapes and sizes can cause shelving problems. They also require equipment for their use. Many libraries provide carrels equipped with power points so that audio-visual equipment can be used. The use of headphones with audio equipment ensures that other library users are not disturbed.

Some of the multi-media items listed above will be quite familiar but others may need further description and explanation.

Films

Commercially produced films are 16 mm and require a 16 mm cine projector. The newer projectors are self-threading which makes things easier for the projectionist. Home-produced films are usually 8 mm and require an 8 mm projector.

Filmloops

A filmloop is a short length of film enclosed in a cassette and with the end of the film spliced on to the beginning so that it requires no rewinding. Filmloops are commercially produced and usually deal with one precise topic.

Filmstrips

A filmstrip is a continuous length of 35 mm film containing a consecutive series of frames. They may be full-frame (equivalent in size to a 35 mm slide) or half frame. Most filmstrip projectors incorporate a masking device for showing half-frame strips. After use the filmstrip has to be rewound ready for the next showing.

Videotapes/videocassettes

In appearance a videotape is like an ordinary magnetic tape such as that used on an open-spool tape recorder. However,

Figure 4 A National Panasonic video recorder

a videotape reproduces visual images as well as sound. Videocassettes are similar but the magnetic tape is completely
enclosed in a cassette and therefore is not handled directly
by the user. Television programmes may be recorded (subject
to copyright regulations) and played back at a later time
using a television monitor. Video is greatly used in schools
and colleges.

Overhead projection (OHP) transparencies
The overhead projector allows the teacher to project information or illustrations on to a screen behind him while he
remains facing the class. In direct use, the overhead projector can replace the chalkboard. The teacher writes or
draws directly on to the acetate roll covering the glass platen
of the projector using a water-based pen. The roll can be
wiped clean after use and re-used. On the other hand, the
teacher may use pre-prepared acetate sheets, either home-
produced using a spirit-based pen to ensure permanence, or
produced on various kinds of document copying machines or
purchased from a commercial firm. The latter are often
beautifully coloured and of very high quality. Librarians
may keep stocks of pre-prepared OHP transparencies which
they have classified, catalogued and made available for
loan.

Kits

School libraries usually stock a variety of kits. They are normally boxes containing samples covering, for example, the production of cotton from its plant stages through to finished cloth.

Handouts

These are duplicated notes distributed by a teacher to his class which cover the main points of a lecture or lesson and replace or supplement the student's/pupil's own notes.

Further information on resource centre equipment, including reprographic machines and methods, may be found in chapter 12, and the storage of software is covered in chapter 7.

Bibliography

British librarianship and information work 1976-1980 edited by L J Taylor. Library Association, 1982.

Butcher, David *Official publications in Britain.* Bingley, 1983.

Cabeceiras, J *The multimedia library.* 2nd ed. Academic Press, 1982.

Dority, G K *Guide to reference books for small and medium-sized libraries, 1970-82.* Libraries Unlimited, 1983.

Dove, J *The audio-visual.* Deutsch, 1975.

Education & Science, Dept. of *Future development of libraries and information services.* HMSO, 1982.

Fothergill, Richard *Non-book materials in libraries: a practical guide.* 2nd ed. Bingley, 1984.

Guide to reference sources for the small library. Hatrics, 1981.

Guidelines for reference and information services to public libraries in England and Wales. Library Association, 1981.

Houghton, Bernard *Online information retrieval systems: an introductory manual . . .* 2nd ed. Bingley, 1984.

Katz, William A *Introduction to reference work* Vols. 1 and 2. 4th ed. McGraw-Hill, 1982.

Online searching: an introduction. Butterworth, 1980.

Prestel in the library context . . . edited by Anna Sheldon. British Library, 1982.

Rowley, J E *Computers for libraries.* Bingley, 1980.

Teague, S J *Microform librarianship.* 2nd ed. Butterworth, 1979.

Walford, A J *Concise guide to reference material.* Library Association, 1981.

Assignments

Written

1 Name *three* bibliographies which cover British publications and write short notes about *each*.
2 List and describe the various guides to British government publications.
3 What information can be found in the following types of publication? In each case, name a reference work as an example:
   (a) almanac
   (b) biographical dictionary
   (c) concordance
   (d) etymological dictionary
   (e) gazetteer
4 List *ten* works of reference which one would expect to find in a library's *quick reference collection*.
5 What is the difference between an index to periodicals and an abstracting journal? Name and describe *one* example of *each*.
6 There are several types of dictionary. Describe *four* different types and cite an example of each.
7 List the types of audio-visual materials which might be stocked by a large library/resource centre. Assess the reasons why libraries stock audio-visual materials.

Practical

1 Go to your local reference library and locate a copy of each of the following reference works. Thoroughly peruse each one and then write short notes *describing* and *evaluating two* of the works listed:

   (a) *Brewer's dictionary of phrase and fable*
   (b) *Fiction index*
   (c) *Granger's index to poetry*
   (d) *Oxford book of quotations*
   (e) *Roget's thesaurus*
   (f) *Sequels*
   (g) *Whitaker's almanack*
   (h) *Willing's press guide*

2 Information retrieval exercise
   Write the answer to each question in the 'answer' column and give the name of the reference book you used in each

case in the 'source' column. Use a different reference work for each question:

Number	Question	Answer	Source
1	Name the oldest, extant castle in Britain.		
2	Name one British library which subscribes to the periodical *Graphics World*.		
3	Of which constituency is Mr Norman St John Stevas the MP?		
4	What is meant by the phrase 'a dog in the manger'?		
5	What does the acronym LADSIRLAC stand for?		
6	Which school did the Rt Hon. Margaret Thatcher attend?		
7	Who wrote the book *Pathways for Communication: books and libraries in the information age*?		
8	Ray Gosling wrote an article about public lending right entitled 'Bye-bye, wilderness: hello, high-tech'. In which periodical did this appear?		
9	Give the author, title, publisher and publication date of any book about the history of cricket from 1890 to 1914.		
10	What is the English equivalent of the German word *Frühling*?		
11	To which tribe did the Biblical character Gideon belong?		
12	Give three other words which have the same meaning as 'restitution'.		

Number	Question	Answer	Source
13	What are the Christian names (forenames) of the composer Tchaikovsky, and how old was he when he died?		
14	What is the maximum size of a cricket bat?		
15	The disease 'rickets' is caused by a deficiency of two things. What are they?		
16	Who wrote: 'A traveller by the faithful hound, Half-buried in the snow was found'?		
17	What is the meaning of the proof correction symbol 'w.f.'?		
18	Where is the headquarters of the World Health Organization?		
19	Of what larger company is the Tetley Tea Co. a subsidiary?		
20	What is the correct way to address an envelope to the Archbishop of Canterbury? (Only the heading need be given, not the full postal address.)		

Chapter Nine

Services to library users

Libraries do not exist in a vacuum. They are provided, and paid for, with some specific objectives in mind. The librarian has a responsibility to provide his service in the most convenient place for his customers and then to make sure that the facilities provided are used. All this implies that the user has expectations and that the librarian must design the service to accommodate them. We all have information or cultural needs and in most towns the library is the best organization to meet these needs. The same is true for special libraries: every member of the organization will have needs that the library could, and should, satisfy. The ambition of the librarian must be to identify the needs in good time, to have the service available at an appropriate point and to encourage the user to approach the library. The objective of this chapter is to look

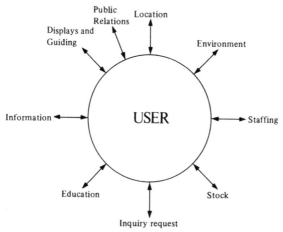

Figure 1 The service and the user

at the factors that make up a service to users. Figure 1 shows the broad headings that will be used, but also note the two-way flow, indicated by the arrows. Only by taking account of users' views can the service be married to the actual changing needs.

Location

Library services are offered through a diverse range of outlets. Rural services are provided by mobile libraries or by small collections in village halls or community centres. Many small towns have branch libraries with opening hours ranging from less than one day a week to full-time. Larger towns may have regional libraries that act as centres for the provision of reference services, inter-library loans, staffing expertise and stock exchange. Major towns may have not only headquarters libraries, but also smaller branch and mobile libraries bringing the service within reach of all the community.

A similar pattern can be seen in non-public libraries. Often academic institutions will have site libraries, supported by a central library. Industrial libraries in larger firms may be in one location, but often each research laboratory will have its own smaller library as well as being able to call upon the parent library.

In schools the same pattern can be seen with classroom libraries and main libraries often operating in the same school.

This multiplicity of provision is both a strength and a weakness for libraries. The cases for centralized versus decentralized provision can be summarized as follows:

Decentralized
1   *Material close at hand.* The user does not have to make too great an effort to obtain service. A motto of public libraries used to be that nobody should be more than half a mile from a service point.
2   *Being smaller they are less overpowering.* It is easier to 'get to know' how things work.
3   *Greater user identity.* Small being beautiful in this case means an easy identification with the location, personnel and materials. In academic libraries teachers talk about 'my books', in industrial libraries researchers get used to working with one particular information officer, etc.

Centralized

1 *Wider range of materials.* Less duplication means that money goes further and buys a wider range of subject cover.

2 *Better 'hit' rate.* More material means that the user has a better chance of finding what he wants without waiting for materials to arrive from other libraries.

3 *More expertise available.* By centralizing stock and staff it is possible for everyone to have access to a wider range of staff expertise.

4 *Better opening hours.* Another staffing function improved by having fewer places to serve. Thus opening hours can be longer and include weekend provision.

Regardless of the decisions prompted by the foregoing, the physical relationship of the building to user access needs detailed consideration. Public libraries have for many years sought out sites in shopping centres or near transport terminals. This is to ensure that their service is easily seen and approached by potential as well as actual users. Much the same consideration affects other libraries — will people walk up or down stairs, across quadrangles, etc just to visit the library? Observation tells us that for many people the least obstacle to easy access will be used as an excuse for not visiting the library. Therefore careful siting is an important factor when considering the way the service will be used.

Environment

It is not enough just to put the library in the best location. Internally it must be conducive to the purpose for which it was intended. Some of the chief factors that we consider when planning the layout of a library are:

1 *Lighting, heating and ventilation*

A fresh, well lit library gives an inviting atmosphere to the public and provides good conditions for staff. Because of book stacks the light may be artificial, but this is acceptable if it is designed properly and does not throw shadows onto the stacks.

2 *Entrance area*

Some modern public libraries have a reception area that would do justice to good hotels. Spacious, well

staffed, carpeted, decorated with floral displays — it wel-
comes the user. The reception area must also act as a
control area to prevent theft and therefore a careful flow
pattern needs to be designed.

3   *Stacks*
Large libraries tend to use an alcoved arrangement to
give a feeling of homeliness. Often these can be developed
into subject libraries with specialist staff operating nearby.
In less difficult times the height of stacks was only two
metres so that all could easily reach the top shelf. The
bottom shelf was never closer to the floor than 50 centimetres. We have now introduced 'kik-steps' and similar
aids and raised the height of shelving somewhat — bottom
shelves are now often at ground level. Many libraries
planned to keep much stock in a reserve collection, not
open to the public. Here shelves were close together and
much higher than in the public areas. Where the service
is offered from more than one floor ease of access needs
consideration. Escalators, lifts and staircases may be
called for to help people to reach the levels easily.

4   *Leisure and study areas*
Every library needs a space with formal and informal
tables and chairs so that users can sit down and consider
the materials they are selecting. In some types of libraries
the study area is of great importance since users will be
spending several hours each day working in the library.

5   *Machine/equipment area*
Many libraries offer booths in which audio and video
materials can be used. The provision of photocopy
machines is now almost universally accepted as standard.
These 'noisy' services need to be carefully located to keep
to a minimum noise transmission to other parts of the
building. One library we know of plays music from its
record department in all the lending areas to help mask
other noise!

6   *Lecture/committee rooms*
Larger libraries will consider lecture rooms an essential
provision for teaching or cultural activities. Often committee rooms are associated with libraries and these can
be hired out to local groups.

Staffing

Once a library is open its development is to a large degree subject to the ability and enthusiasm of its staff. They have a crucial role to play if the library is to seek out and supply the services needed by its users.

Patterns of staffing vary a lot according to the type of library. In many public libraries a picture of 1:1 professional to non-professional staff mix emerges. This is also true of some academic libraries. In industrial, commercial or professional libraries the proportion of professional staff will increase substantially. Here it is the pattern of use that dictates the staffing. Much of the work of these special libraries is giving direct assistance to the user, doing research, producing summaries, etc. The volume of stock to be processed, shelved or issued is therefore much less than in public libraries.

Professional staff in all types of libraries will be drawn from a wide range of subject backgrounds. Increasingly they take first degrees in a major subject and support this with postgraduate librarianship qualifications. When in post their titles will vary widely — information officer, subject librarian, research officer, tutor-librarian being some examples. Even in public libraries the range of titles increases each year — regional librarian, divisional librarian, training officer, special services librarian, community librarian being added to the traditional branch, reference, children's, central, cataloguing librarians we have grown used to seeing.

These new titles are not just cosmetic, they do reflect the ever-changing role of the library service and its place in the community it serves. They also reflect the increasing specialization of services that every type of library is seeking to offer. From the small school library to the largest county library each is handling a wider range of materials and a diverse range of information services. To do this the staff need to be of a high quality and carefully selected.

Stock

We have written elsewhere about the importance of providing a balanced stock of up-to-date materials. Under this heading we need only add the importance of displaying it attractively, keeping it in good order and repair and ensuring that an adequate level of duplication is provided to meet peak demands.

Its division into subject collections must be considered, eg reference, children's, adult, fiction, as must the possibility of integrating all *forms* of materials into one sequence. The problems are many — but so are the benefits.

Inquiry/request service

Dealing with inquiries is part of the role of the qualified member of staff. It is an essential user service and provides the cornerstone to the efficient use of the library. All the things that follow in the chapter are subservient to the inquiry point and its proper manning.

In many libraries there will be a number of these service desks, usually located near the part of the collection they offer special help in exploiting. The concept of the subject collection is common to most types of library. Perhaps national, industrial and academic libraries have developed it to its fullest extent, but most large public libraries will have a 'technical librarian', 'music librarian', etc. In the more developed pattern you will see 'law librarian', 'planning librarian', etc and these posts will probably be linked to a teaching function in an academic library or a research function in industrial libraries.

Their special qualifications will involve not only a knowledge of the bookstock in the subject and the bibliographical aids but also the whole range of materials that are currently produced. They will also know about the subject itself and will thus be able to offer advice to users in a more detailed fashion than the 'general' readers' adviser.

It follows from this that they will be recommending materials not necessarily available in the stock of the library. So they will also be involved in the provision of request services. These will, of course, be part of a unified service for the whole library once the specialist has done the bibliographic work.

The whole problem of inter-library loans and internal request services is dealt with in Chapter Six, but we must make the point here that we librarians have a professional duty to ensure that our readers are made aware of materials not currently available in the library yet obtainable by purchase or loan. Remember that to most people the stock they see on the shelves represents everything you can offer them. We must put that right by personal intervention and help.

Teaching/educational role

Part of the role of any librarian who works with users is quite clearly educational. The training in the use of catalogues, bibliographies, reference books, etc that a readers' adviser gives as part of his normal duties is an educational function if properly performed. We are occasionally shocked still to hear users being told, 'You'll find that over there on the left.' This type of help gives the user no insight into the arrangement and organization of knowledge as reflected in that library. Move the stock round and he is lost again!

So our job, done professionally, involves education at a basic level. We develop this by working alongside users in assembling a 'package' of materials to satisfy their inquiry.

In academic libraries the formal commitment to teach is much clearer, many librarians being employed as lecturing staff and operating for much of their time in class or tutorial rooms and, of course, conducting tutorials from the special subject inquiry desks. They are also employed in assisting with the development of new courses of study.

The public librarian has another 'educational' role. This is the offering of special lecture programmes as part of the cultural life of the area. In some libraries, theatres and museums, etc form a part of the overall cultural provision.

Librarians of all sorts are invited to speak to local groups — Young Wives, Women's Guilds, Rotary, etc — about their job and the services the modern library provides. Each of these occasions is a contribution to the education of the audience — or at least it ought to be so viewed!

Information services

Most librarians see their role as active providers of information rather than adopting a 'we are here, come and use us' attitude. This professional approach leads us into making judgements about what information is
1   required by whom,
2   how quickly,
3   in what form,
4   in what detail,
5   from which sources.
   Taking these in order we must first assess:
1   Who wants what information. At a simplistic level the production of a list of authors who write on a particular

subject meets these criteria. It is produced for a group of readers who constantly ask the librarian, 'Who else writes war stories?' What they want is a list of authors that they can consult when browsing.

At the other end of this scale librarians seek out profiles of the subject interests of individual users and produce annotated lists of books, journals, reports, standards, patents, etc that appear on the topics to be covered.

How do we find out what people need to know? The best way is to talk to them, using a structured plan so that you do get round to asking the right questions. In some cases a questionnaire is circulated to gather the information.

Many specialist librarians find they deal only with the final user. Research has shown that many people get their 'updates' from someone called 'the gatekeeper'. These individuals are found in many companies and they are the type of person to whom members of a company refer to each other. 'Go and ask Harry, he reads all those reports.' The librarian can also tap this network and direct current awareness information to 'the gatekeeper'!

2 Sound judgement is needed to assess the speed with which the information is required. If you provide too much too often you achieve overkill; too little and you make no impact. Obviously, if you receive a document about safety and your company makes the equipment concerned a phone call is indicated. If you are drawing attention to recently acquired journals or books a weekly or monthly listing could be considered enough. Many libraries provide users with photocopies of contents pages of selected journals; this selective dissemination of information (SDI) service will require that the copy be sent on the day the journal arrives.

In public libraries guides to the literature of various subjects are produced. Here the speed with which they need to be made available can only be decided by the librarian.

3 The form of presentation can be important. If it looks attractive and different there is an inclination to pick it up and read it. The same old cover year after year leads to 'It's only the libraries . . .' comment. Often you will

need to circulate the actual document or a copy of it and then some monitoring of its progress round the addresses is required. It is surprising how these things can sit on a desk for weeks, even *after* they have been read.

Traditionally, libraries sent out typed and duplicated or printed copy, but increasingly photocopies of parts of the original are used in academic and industrial libraries. It is of interest that the use of microforms is increasing. With the spread of library catalogues on fiche, etc it is common to find microfiche readers and catalogues scattered around an organization. This leaves the way open for general current awareness services (CAS) to be offered in this form also. Some libraries provide information within their parent organization via computer terminals and the main computer. Daily, even hourly, updates of information can be fed into the computer and users can call it up on their nearest terminal or VDU. Links between distant parts of a system can be made using standard computer links or the new Viewdata standards.

4   The amount of detail required depends on the individual case. It can range, as we have said, from a list of authors to the circulation of the full original. In most libraries some author, title and subject arrangement is augmented by a brief annotation giving the user an indication of content, level and anything of particular concern to the organization. In some cases a fuller abstract will be needed. The judgement of the librarian has to be exercised in each case, so that an information bulletin may consist of a mixture of recent additions, photocopies of reviews, contents pages, abstracts of key articles, listings of other articles and perhaps photocopies of computer print-outs.

5   What sources do we use? In Chapter Ten we talk about many of the services librarians use to obtain information. We have mentioned above the original work in abstracting and indexing that a librarian may undertake from the materials within his own collections. To these we must add the increasing power of on-line computer searchings.

Within the heading of on-line systems we want to look at three quite separate systems. These are Teletext, Viewdata and traditional on-line computer systems.

Teletext

Teletext is provided by the BBC and IBA and is broadcast as part of their television services. This information service is only available when television programmes or test cards are being transmitted, which means that the BBC2 service and Channel 4 are sometimes not available until the late afternoon. The special sets for receiving the Teletext information are provided with hand control units on which you can select the desired pages of the system. When you key in a page on one of the control units, you will see the page number selected in the upper left-hand corner of the screen. Next to it you will see the page number currently being received and this will change while the set seeks out the page you have dialled, which may take several seconds.

Several hundred pages of information are available on each channel, concerned mainly with current news events, weather, sporting news, retail prices, share prices and amusement.

This information has the great advantage, as mentioned previously, of being free to the user and of being updated quickly and efficiently by research staff at the BBC and IBA. For example, news pages on CEEFAX are updated every day. The service on BBC2 tends to deal with more serious material in greater depth, while BBC1 concentrates on current news, sports and business matters. ORACLE, the IBA service, is provided to all of the ITV companies. It generally provides two types of information: pages in the 100 sequence provide news, sport and current events while pages in the 300 sequence provide news of interest to the region. At the time of writing not all regions are covered by the 300 page sequence. Channel 4 operates its own service using pages 400 and 500 and while covering major news items seeks to supplement the information available on the ITV channels with more consumer-based information as well as details of its own programmes.

Viewdata

Viewdata-Prestel provides, in effect, an electronic reference library. Because there is no need to send data for the whole set of pages, as the Teletext systems must, it becomes possible to provide an enormous database. A suitable terminal to receive Prestel is necessary. This combines a TV set and a telephone. Normally the individual user will dial and gain access to a Viewdata centre in his local telephone area. As a result, his telephone charges will be for a local call. The user has a simple keypad, having the numbers 0 to 9 and * and buttons with which to interact with the computer. The computer offers the user multiple choices (selected by number) at each stage of a search for information, leading him through a tree structure to the required item. It is also possible to use an alphanumeric keypad which allows access to the newly-created facilities offered by the introduction of the 'Gateway' and 'Mailbox' services.

'Gateway' allows links to be established between your television and other Viewdata or computer systems.

'Mailbox' allows you to send messages to other Prestel users and these messages will be displayed automatically when they next access Prestel.

The special TV set contains a decoder which translates the data signals sent by the computer and displays them on the screen.

The information on Prestel is provided by numerous individual 'information providers' as they are called. These may be commercial firms, government bodies, educational institutions or any other group which desires to put information on the system and is willing to pay to do so. Although they are charged for putting information on Prestel, they are allowed to set their own charges for each page of information provided. These charges range from 0 to 50p per page. In addition, some information providers, such as Infotex, charge an annual fee to users for special pass numbers which will give them access to the providers' pages.

Two drawbacks of the Prestel service are firstly that the information providers update their own material and some do this very infrequently so that the user gets much out-of-date information, and secondly that the printed indexes provided are difficult to use and do not give enough detail, resulting in lengthy and sometimes circuitous searches for required information. This obviously increases the cost of using the service.

It is also unfortunate that most receivers are still provided with numeric, not alphanumeric, keyboards, thereby limiting and slowing down the intercommunication between computer and user, and that most receivers are not connected to printers. However, it is now possible to purchase sets whch do have alphanumeric keyboards and to which printers are attached, although these sets are much more expensive.

Information available on Prestel of particular relevance to libraries includes:

1   Specific legal data provided for the profession by a specialized information provider, eg labour law updates, information on legal aid and advice, consumer law updates, tax guide, European tax guide, latest proceedings in Parliament and the European Parliament, recent case reports, etc.

2   Commercial information about companies, provided by Fintel, Dunn and Bradstreet, the Stock Exchange, etc.

3   Useful information of a more general kind, eg British Rail timetables, news, weather, currency exchange rates, government statistics, etc.

4   A new method of accessing the Prestel system was launched in February 1983 and is in effect a low cost version of Prestel aimed at the home computer user and the small business micros. Now instead of buying a special Prestel television it is possible to convert many models of micro and personal computers to act as though they were a full colour Prestel terminal. Micronet 800 sell an adaptor which allows the telephone to be connected to the micro through which access to the full range of Prestel pages is available. Part of the special provision gained by using this particular method of accessing Prestel is that it is now possible to down load computer programmes through the Micronet 800 link. Many of these programmes are available free of charge and once down loaded can be used on the microcomputer used to access the Prestel service. Obviously once down loaded the telephone line is closed off and the microcomputer acts as a normal microcomputer should.

On-line information retrieval systems

The advantages of these systems are:

1   Very large databases, containing details of many, many more periodical articles, indexes, abstracts, texts, dissertations, reports, statutes and so on than any library except the largest could hope to have in its stock.

2   The great speed at which the computer can scan and sort enormous quantities of material.

3   The rapid updating of databases, usually much more quickly than the material entered on the bases could be

published by conventional means. To take one example of this, consider the Finance Act 1980, which has 122 sections and 20 schedules. It took the government printer over a month after the Act had been passed to publish the raw text by conventional means. Because of the speed and flexibility of telepublishing, the Lexis system was able to include the Act on its database, incorporating all amendments and deletions together with editorial annotation, only 22 days after receipt of the text. For the first time, the whole of the statute book will be made available and continuously kept up to date in its current state, indicating the date every part came or comes into force, incorporating all relevant statutory instruments and annotated throughout.

4   Meticulous checking of the material as it is put on to the databases, to ensure complete accuracy.

5   Great flexibility of approach — that is, the variety of ways in which material can be acted upon. For example, on the legal databases, the user can retrieve a case by the judges' names, the counsels' names, or by keying in any relevant words in the text.

Examples of on-line services are:

1   *DIALOG* (Lockheed Information Systems). Over 200 bases, mainly bibliographical with abstracts covering most of the world's major subjects.

2   *BLAISE*, which includes bibliographical records for monographs and first editions of serials published in the United Kingdom and the United States, as well as records of audio-visual materials. It now has the British Education Index available.

3   *TEXTLINE*, a precis of business news from major daily newspapers and weekly journals.

4   *E.S.A*, a European host offering some 35 major scientific bases.

5   *DataStar*, offering a mixture of business, scientific and technical information.

6   *POLIS*, the on-line service covering Parliament. It is produced by the Library of the House of Commons and is updated overnight to cover each day's debates. Currently *Hansard* is being put on-line in full text.

7 *Infoline,* similar to 1 above but UK based.

8 *EUROLEX*, which at present contains the following 'libraries', as they are called:

Common Market Law Reports 1962—
Fleet Street Reports 1963—
Times Law Reports 1976—
Weekly Law Reports 1970—
European Human Rights Reports 1979—
European Commercial Cases 1978—
Current Law Yearbook 1977—
Current Law Monthly 1980—
Statutes in Force
Reports of Patent Cases 1970—
Council of Europe Treaties 1948—
European Law Digest 1973—

9 *LEXIS*, has these 'libraries':

The Law Reports 1945—
The All England Law Reports 1945—
Weekly Law Reports 1953—
Lloyd's List Law Reports 1945—
Public General Acts on Revenue Law, Industrial Law, Company and Partnership Law, Law of Landlord and Tenant
(Statutes on other areas of the law are to be added so that the whole field of statute law is covered within three years)
The Statutory Instruments for each subject area will be made available at the same time as the corresponding Statutes
United Kingdom Tax Library
United States Libraries of Federal and State Statutes and Case Law

10 *LAWTEL,* a legal information retrieval service on PRESTEL. This is a 'closed user group' which means you pay an annual subscription but get free page access via PRESTEL. The service allows daily updates of changes proposed in the law, the state of enactment and progress through Parliament.

Taken in conjunction with EUROLEX and LEXIS it provides an almost complete package of on-line legal information.

In Figure 2 we show a typical example of a Dialog search.
You will see that we search for the effects of the computer
on society. In this simple example search terms like society,
microprocessors, etc were entered singly and given a 'set'
number by the computer. Under the heading 'items' the
computer lists the total number of articles to be found
containing that single term. By combining the various set
numbers it is possible to narrow the search to produce a particular result. You will notice in set 9 terms 7 and 8 have been
called for and a result of 2814 items was found. In set 10
the two terms were both accepted, ie 7 *or* 8 and this increased
the number of articles found to over 65,000. A specimen
page of the printout is given in Figure 3. The search was
carried out on an educational base (ERIC) and so reflects
the problem from the stand point of the education service.
A search on a technological or computer base would have
produced a totally different set of references. It is, therefore,
important when practising on-line searching not only to
formulate the search terms carefully but also to select the
base upon which the search will be run with equal care. The
two forms in Figure 4 show typical aids in mapping out a
search strategy.

```
User  6907    Date:28feb80    Time: 9:47:01    File:  1

Set Items Description
  1 14209 SOCIETY
  2    29 MICROPROCESSOR?
  3 13833 COMPUTER?
  4   312 COMPUTER(W)TECHNOLOGY
  5    29 MICROPROCESSOR?
  6 13834 2-5/OR
  7  8700 IMPACT
  8 5 188 EFFECT?
  9  2814 7AND8
 10 65074 7OR8
 11   132 1AND6AND10

Print 11/3/11-132

Search Time:  0.225   Prints: 122   Descs.:   8
```

*Figure 2   DIALOG search: the effects of the computer on
society*

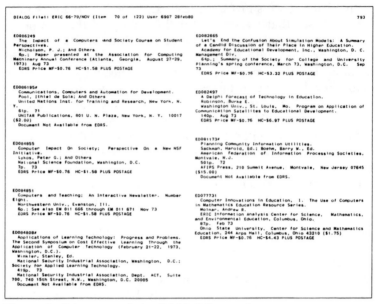

Figure 3 Print-out of the DIALOG search

One of the great truths about computers, or any other form of information searching, is 'rubbish in, rubbish out'. Ask silly questions and you get silly answers. The skilled searcher will spend much time with the inquirer defining what is really wanted, getting examples of references already found that are good, sorting out the language of the subject. This is time well invested since it saves money in the end and leads to a higher success rate in providing information.

Displays

The physical location of a library branch, in some convenient centre, has often been considered the best form of display to attract users to the service. Now librarians are also adopting a more direct approach to 'selling' their services.

Display techniques are considered in two parts, external and internal.

Purposes of external display

1   To widen the library's sphere of influence and service.
2   To stimulate interest in books and reading.

On-line Service			Search Outline	

TOPIC

SELECT SETS

1	2	3	4	5

COMBINE SETS

ON-LINE PRINTS   **OFF-LINE PRINTS**

COSTS

(i)   Telecommunications   All _____ / _____ P.O. _____ / _____
(ii) Database _____
(iii) U.K. call charges _____

TOTAL SEARCH COST _____

on-line information retrieval system

CHELMER

Essex Institute of Higher Education

Requestor . . . .

References: List authors of any relevant papers already known to you

Department/Organisation . . . .

Address . . . .
. . . .

Keywords: suggest subject terms in your own vocabulary

Telephone: . . . .

Subject — please state as specifically as possible

Limitations

1. Maximum number of references required . . . .
if fewer than . . . . found broaden search
Suggested broader subject . . . .
. . . .

BACKGROUND — give any mechnical background information necessary to clarify your enquiry

2. Time — Any limits on date required:
. . . .

3. Date bases — please state any special instructions, regarding choice:
. . . .
. . . .

Departmental Approval by . . . .
. . . .

Figure 4 Two standard aids to computer searching

3   To attract non-members and encourage them to join the library.
4   To catch the eye of the uninterested. People who will not stop to read pamphlets, brochures, etc produced by the library may be arrested by an eye-catching, colourful display.
5   To show what information is available in print, and in other media such as gramophone records, filmstrips, etc on topics of current interest.

Methods of external display
1   Use of shop windows. Co-operation with shop manager to produce a display of shop goods plus relevant books on an agreed theme.
2   Use of billboards and advertising space on local transport. Colourful posters can draw attention to the library's services, to special events like National Book Week, to extra-mural activities such as story hours, etc.
3   Provision of display cases near the library entrance or display windows around the external walls. Librarians should promote the library's stock and services by attractive display in the same way that shopkeepers promote their sales.

Purposes of internal display
1   To make the library environment more attractive and more welcoming.
2   To relieve the monotony of rows and rows of books in strict author (fiction) or classified (non-fiction) order.
3   To make library members more aware of their library's resources and facilities.
4   To draw attention to certain areas of stock which are under-used. Money and time are wasted when books sit on library shelves week after week and are never looked at or borrowed.
5   To bring together in a temporary display books on related topics which are otherwise permanently separated by the classification scheme. For example, a display entitled 'Parent and Child' could bring together books from 155.4: child psychology; 370: education; 392: customs connected with child rearing; 613.9: birth control.

6   To display material in one department which is normally housed in another department.

7   To try to widen readers' interests and tastes in books. For example, one can try to influence the person who reads only non-fiction by drawing his attention to fictional books on the same theme, or vice versa. A display of books on France can include guidebooks, maps, books on French art, music, cookery, etc plus fictional books set in France or books by French novelists.

8   To let readers see the latest additions to stock before they are shelved in correct sequence and thereby 'hidden'.

Methods of internal display

1   Use of display boards and fittings between bookcases to relieve monotony.

2   Use of permanent display area with glass showcases, etc, eg in library's foyer.

3   Use of temporary, movable display stands.

4   Use of plastic jackets to lengthen life of paper dust jackets. This helps to keep stock clean, colourful and attractive.

5   Use of dust jackets wrapped around dummy books for displays behind glass. This ensures that the books themselves are available for loan.

Problems arising from display

1   Books on display are missing from the shelves. Serious readers searching for books on a topic at the appropriate class number will overlook those on display.

2   Readers obviously want to borrow books on display so either
    (a) the display has to be constantly modified as books are borrowed,
    (b) the reader has to reserve books on display and wait till the entire display is dismantled,
    (c) book jackets must be used in displays and not the books themselves, thus freeing books for loan, or
    (d) extra copies must be purchased to satisfy increased demand.

3   Good display necessitates staff skilled in artwork, lettering, etc. It is also time consuming.

Suggested topics for display
1   National and international events.
2   Commemorative occasions.
3   Social problems.
4   Topics of local interest.
5   Seasonal topics.
6   Hobbies and handicrafts.
7   Specific subjects.
8   Recent additions to stock.
9   Display linked to a 'service', eg request service.

Points to avoid
1   Amateurish displays.
2   Poor lettering.
3   Poor use of colour.
4   Inadequate lighting.
5   Books with dull covers (perhaps display books open to show a colourful illustration).
6   Haphazard arrangement.
7   Displays not changed often enough.

Guiding
Types of library guiding
1   Catalogue
2   Plan
3   Class guides
4   Tier guides
5   Shelf guides
6   Topic guides
7   Individual book guides
8   Dummy books
9   Printed guide
10 Personal guide

1   *The library catalogue*
    The catalogue is the key to the entire stock of the library. It guides the reader to the location of
    (a) books on a particular subject,
    (b) books by a particular author,
    (c) a particular book where only the title is known.
    (d) books on related topics.
    It does this by providing catalogue entries under subjects,

authors, titles, etc, and by providing references. The location is indicated by the class number given on the catalogue entry and by symbols denoting parallel arrangement, eg the letter 'q' for quarto denoting an oversize book shelved in a separate section because of its size.

In addition the catalogue acts as a guide to individual books by showing on catalogue entries

(a) descriptive information, ie edition, place of publication, publisher, date;

(b) bibliographical information, ie number of pages, whether illustrated, etc;

(c) special features which are mentioned in an annotation.

2 *Plan*

The plan of the library should portray the floor area of the public departments, showing the positions of bookcases with the subjects (or class numbers) of books housed in these bookcases. This plan should be prominently displayed, preferably near the catalogue.

3 *Class guides*

These are placed at the beginning of each class and show the relevant class number and subject. The lettering should be large enough for readers to see it clearly at a distance. When a reader has ascertained from the catalogue the class number of the subject he wants, he must be able to find, on the shelves, without a lot of searching, books with that class number.

4 *Tier guides*

Each separate bookcase or tier should have a guide above the top shelf indicating the contents of that bookcase. The lettering should be clear and bold (usually about 5 centimetres high) and should be movable or easily altered because bookstocks do not remain static. Cork or plastic letters and figures are often used.

5 *Shelf guides*

Shelf guides must be moved as the stock moves and so need fairly constant revision. They indicate the subject coverage of the books on each shelf, or the part of the alphabet covered in the case of fiction books.

6   *Topic guides*

Topic guides are now out of vogue. In years gone by
librarians covered wooden blocks (of book height) with
colourful pictures depicting topics dealt with in the
books shelved alongside. This was at a time when stocks
were not so large, space was not at a premium, and the topic
guides effectively broke the monotony of rows and rows
of dull-looking books. In the present era of plastic jackets,
bookstocks look bright and attractive in themselves.

7   *Individual book guides*

These are class numbers (or author letters) shown on the
spines of books. Lettering should be at a constant height
from the base of the spine to give a uniformity of appearance along a shelf of books. There are many methods of
lettering in use, eg electric stylus, Dymo tape, self-adhesive
labels and indian ink, etc.

8   *Dummy books*

The use of dummy books in guiding is also a thing of the
past. It used to be common practice to keep certain
books in the librarian's office or in a locked cupboard
(eg books on sex), so a dummy book was placed on the
appropriate shelf in its correct class sequence to indicate
to the reader that the original was housed elsewhere but
would be produced on request. Some librarians pains-
takingly made realistic dummy books to the confusion of
not-so-bright readers who wondered why the books
would not open!

Public relations

Public relations begins with that first welcome smile from the
assistant at the counter and runs through the efficient charging and discharging of materials, the general appearance of
the place, the help offered, the stock and the services available. In fact, everything that makes up a modern library
contributes to our good public image.

Senior librarians will have specific responsibilities for
formal public relations, presenting the library's case at committees, talking to residents' groups, etc. They will also be
the people who make decisions on the operation of the
service that can lead to problems for junior staff!

An example of this is when a reduction of services has to be undertaken — for example, withdrawing the reservation of new fiction, or reducing opening hours. It is important that staff, the press, councillors and others are briefed as to why that option was followed rather than any other. By putting forward a good argument it is sometimes possible to turn bad news into a good public relations exercise. We know of several services where a proper and honest explanation to the user has led to the controlling body restoring cuts or increasing provision. People do have power!

No amount of pre-planning will eliminate all complaints and a proper procedure needs to be created to handle these problems. We do not want to see young assistants at the counter getting involved in an argument. Therefore two things are required. First, the assistant must know who is the senior person to whom to take the problem. Second, an office must be available in which to conduct the interview.

The customer may not always be right, but we feel he has a right to express a point of view, and as librarians we have a duty to consider his complaint seriously. We must also explain what steps are possible to rectify the problem. These may be drawn from a list such as this:

1 Approach their councillor/manager.
2 Make an appointment to see the chief librarian.
3 Offer a compromise solution — waive the fine, issue an extra ticket, etc.
4 Give an assurance that an investigation will be made and that a report will be sent in due course — often the best approach when staffing problems are involved.
5 Explain why a particular rule is necessary and how it helps maintain the service.

Public relations, then, has four facets:

1 Relations with providing body.
2 Relations with users.
3 Relations with potential users.
4 Relations with library staff.

Each is built upon the reputation being created by the service and so all staff have a duty to enhance and develop the quality of what they do within the limits of their responsibilities. They must be active in bringing forward suggestions from users of ways in which the service could be improved, and in seeking reasons from users and non-users for using or not using the services.

Some libraries go to great lengths to assess consumer response to their services. Whole areas of a town may be questioned, local newspapers may run a feature and encourage readers' letters, staff may interview within the library on the random 'Gallop' principle. This collection and analysis of information will help to plan a better service and so give the user something nearer to what he wants. The best form of public relations is a satisfied user.

Bibliography
Burkett, S and others *Library practice*. Elm, 1977.
Lock, R N *Manual of library economy*. London, Bingley, 1977. Part II.

Written assignments
1   Give a detailed account of two readers' services offered in your library. Compare one of them with a similar service in another library.
2   Describe how a reader's inquiry is answered in your library, assuming that it starts at the issue desk.
3   Produce a topic for a current awareness publication. Give the headings you might use and a few specimen entries under one heading.
4   You are planning a new library in a small town. Briefly describe the factors you would consider in deciding its physical location.
5   Once the library in 4 above is open, what steps would you take to publicize it in the town?
6   Design a form that could be used as a basis for an SDI system in your library.
7   Comment on (a) the purposes *and* (b) the methods of library display and publicity.

Chapter Ten

Library co-operation

From 1850, when the British public library service was born, until the early decades of the twentieth century, each library was an entity, service or trying to serve the needs of its own membership and purchasing books to meet their primary demands. However, a combination of circumstances made it increasingly difficult for an individual library to be self-sufficient. These circumstances included:

1   a tremendous increase in knowledge and a corresponding growth in publishing:
2   the spread of education from primary through to university level which led to greater and more diverse demands on the public library service by a much more literate public;
3   the advance of technology with its effect on industry and commerce and the necessity for employers and employees to develop new skills and techniques;
4   increased opportunities for travel and international economic co-operation which demanded up-to-date information about foreign countries.

These factors altered and increased the demands on the library service. It became impossible for an individual library to meet all the requirements of its own clientele and so the call for organized schemes of library co-operation began to be heard. The loudest call came from the Kenyon report in 1927 which recommended:

1   a system of voluntary co-operation between all types of public library authority whether county, county borough, municipal borough or district;
2   the creation of regional networks based on large urban libraries;

3 co-operation between special libraries, eg industrial, commercial, academic;
4 the creation of a national central library to co-ordinate the entire co-operative system.

The National Central Library came into being in 1931, and by 1937 a system of regional library bureaux had been set up to cover the whole of England and Wales. The problem of discovering what resources were available in the participating libraries was overcome by the production of union catalogues at the bureaux and at the National Central Library. A number of non-public libraries participated in the co-operative scheme and they were known as outlier libraries.

The middle of the twentieth century saw further developments in library co-operation which included schemes for co-operative purchase and subject specialization and for the exchange and redistribution of withdrawn books. The National Lending Library for Science and Technology and the National Reference Library of Science and Invention were set up, both of which are now incorporated into the British Library.

In more recent years the advance of technology has brought major improvements to the networks of library co-operation. These include the use of telex to speed up inter-library loan requests, computerized cataloguing and bibliographic services, the availability of microform editions of union catalogues such as the LASER catalogue (London and South Eastern Regional Library Bureau), and the easy production of photocopies.

The picture may appear rosy but there were some thorns in certain areas. Some of the union catalogues at regional library bureaux were comprehensive and reliable but others were incomplete. Some libraries leaned too heavily on the interloan network and shirked their own responsibility in book purchasing. Also, the heavy demands on the interloan scheme sometimes meant long delays in getting the required material.

The basis of a national inter-library loan network must surely be a co-operative scheme of acquisition and storage. It would be a hit and miss system if one were merely to hope that a requested book might have been bought by some library somewhere in the country. A methodical scheme of co-operative purchase ensures there are no gaps in acquisition and no unnecessary duplication. A degree of duplication is inevitable as each library's first concern must be for its own readers and their demands with regard to stock.

The first of the subject specialization schemes was set up in London in 1948 whereby 28 libraries agreed to specialize in certain subject areas (represented by Dewey classification numbers) so that jointly they would achieve good coverage of all publications on all subjects. The scheme included not only book purchase but the acquisition of withdrawn items from other libraries and the permanent storage of all materials in their allotted subject fields.

A larger scheme based on the South Eastern Regional Library system was inaugurated in 1949 whereby 85 libraries agreed to purchase jointly all books listed in *British National Bibliography*. Other regions followed with similar schemes of co-operative acquisition with the aim of making each region self-sufficient. However, these regional schemes were disbanded when the British Library came into being in 1973.

By law, United Kingdom publishers must submit a free copy of every book published to six designated libraries, including the British Library. These legal deposit copies are therefore available as a back-up to the interloan scheme.

Concurrently with the discontinuation of regional schemes for acquisition and storage of materials came local government reorganization and the incorporation of previously autonomous borough libraries into the appropriate county library systems. County library authorities are therefore much larger and more powerful than they were, and some have initiated their own schemes of acquisition and storage which will make them as self-sufficient as possible.

Co-operative purchase of new publications has to be supplemented by schemes for the acquisition of out-of-print and rare materials. Material discarded by one library may be urgently required by another and some method is required whereby libraries are informed of available items. To co-ordinate this work, the British National Book Centre (BNBC) was set up in 1948. Libraries notified BNBC of their discarded items and lists then circulated to libraries in Britain and later to exchange centres abroad. Foreign materials are also obtained through exchange agreements, principally between the national libraries of the countries concerned.

Local co-operative schemes

Sheffield pioneered the idea of a local co-operative network in the 1930s. The 12 original libraries participating in the scheme have now been joined by more than 50 others and the range includes public, academic, industrial, commercial, research association and chamber of commerce libraries. Co-operation is on a 'give and take' basis with each participating library fulfilling an obligation to subscribe to a minimum number of periodicals and to carry a bookstock of a stipulated minimum size. The organization is entitled the Sheffield Interchange Organization but it is better known by its acronym SINTO. The union catalogue of the holdings of participating libraries is maintained by the Department of Commerce, Science and Technology of Sheffield public library. The backbone of the co-operative venture is the interlending of materials, but their activities have included the monitoring of withdrawn stock, the compilation of a union list of periodicals, the production of several indexes and the sponsoring of information research projects.

Since the formation of SINTO, many other local networks have been set up in various parts of the country. Many of them are known by their acronyms such as CICRIS (Co-operative Industrial and Commercial Reference and Information Service), LADSIRLAC (Liverpool and District Scientific, Industrial and Research Library Advisory Council), and ESSNET, the network based at Essex County Library.

Regional co-operative schemes

Most co-operation at regional level has been channelled through the regional library bureaux. Nine regions were formed and these were Northern, West Midlands, Wales and Monmouth, London and South East, East Midlands, North West, Yorkshire, South West, and Scotland.

Other informal schemes of regional co-operation were set up in various parts of the country. One such network was the Yorkshire Cobook Scheme in which 11 autonomous library authorities agreed to a co-operative book purchasing scheme.

The national network

At the hub of the national network of library co-operation stands the British Library Lending Division (BLLD) in Boston Spa, Yorkshire. It was set up in 1973 by amalgamating the stocks and services of the National Central Library with the National Lending Library for Science and Technology. BLLD is the 'library of last resort' for inter-library loans in that local and regional sources should be tried first before British Library is approached. BLLD has its own vast stock of about 4.5 million books and bound periodicals, 3.5 million documents in microform, along with a vast number of serials, dissertations and reports from which most of its 2.7 million requests per annum can be supplied. In addition BLLD maintains a union catalogue and can trace other sources if its own stock cannot meet the need. The British Library Lending Division publishes a list of its own periodicals holdings entitled *Current Serials Received.* The library subscribes to more than 55,000 periodicals, and also has in stock about 70,000 sets of periodicals which are no longer in publication, so most requests for photocopies of periodical articles can be met from BLLD's own resources. In addition, however, the *British Union Catalogue of Periodicals* gives major locations for a vast number of periodicals.

The British National Book Centre which co-ordinates a national and international scheme for the exchange or redistribution of unwanted stock is also housed in the BLLD buildings at Boston Spa. BNBC is now re-named as the Gift and Exchange Division.

Aslib and special library co-operation

The Association of Special Libraries and Information Bureaux was founded in 1924 by a group of librarians working in research stations. Its present extent includes corporate membership by industrial libraries (about 59 per cent), university and college libraries (about 14 per cent), public libraries (about 11 per cent) and also a sizeable number of personal members (about 16 per cent).

Aslib was influential in the development of several areas of inter-library co-operation, notably the establishment of the National Central Library, the provision of a union catalogue for London libraries, the compilation of location indexes of European and Russian scientific journals, the publication of the *British Union Catalogue of Periodicals* and *British National Bibliography.*

Aslib maintains its own library for use by its members and also administers an interlending service between participating libraries. Other services include panels of translators and indexers on whom members may call, research and consultancy services related to special libraries and the organization of courses on various aspects of information work. Aslib's publications include the *Aslib directory* and the *Index to theses*.

Bibliography

Acronyms and abbreviations in library and information work. 2nd ed. London, Library Association, 1982.

Harrod, L M *Librarians' glossary of terms used in librarianship, documentation and the book crafts and reference book.* 5th ed. London, Gower, 1984.

Jefferson, G *Library co-operation.* 2nd ed. London, Deutsch, 1977.

Katz, W A *Introduction to reference work,* vol 2, 4th ed. McGraw-Hill, 1982.

Martin, S K *Library networks,* 1981-82. Knowledge Industry, 1981.

Plaister, J M *Computing in LASER: regional library co-operation.* Library Association, 1982.

Assignments

Practical

Discover the extent of participation of your library (ie the one in which you work or of which you are a member) in local, regional and national networks of library co-operation.

Written

1   Write brief notes on the following:
    (a) British Library Lending Division
    (b) Aslib
    (c) regional library bureaux
2   What are the full names of the organizations represented by the following acronyms?
    (a) CICRIS
    (b) LADSIRLAC
    (c) NANTIS
    (d) SCONUL
3   What are the advantages of:
    (a) co-operative acquisition and storage of materials?
    (b) union catalogues and union lists of periodicals?
    (c) the inter-library loan scheme?

Chapter Eleven

Understanding the purposes, uses and production of library publications

There is no doubt that libraries are part of the 'communications industry'; simply by providing an information service they qualify for that definition. The role of libraries in communication goes much further than simply answering questions, however.

Many libraries attempt to predict their users' questions and have material ready for sale, or hand-outs to answer them. We have already considered several examples of this prediction of inquiries, for example:
1   libraries know that new members will want information about their services and so produce a reader's guide that can be taken away and studied at leisure;
2   to help with their general education programme libraries often produce displays on topics of current concern and support these with reading lists;
3   library members' attention is drawn to new material with lists of recent additions to stock;
4   posters are produced advertising special activities;
5   libraries keep specialists up to date by publishing reviews of the literature in specific subject areas and circulating copies;
6   guides are published to periodicals either held by a library or by a group of co-operating libraries;
7   some libraries extend their range of publishing to cover local history pamphlets, consumer news sheets, etc, thus being publishers in the truest sense of the word.
These are just a few of the uses librarians have for producing publications; you should be able to look round your own library and add several others. It is a good bet that

if asked why libraries produce so much material of this type the librarian would answer by saying that it all helps members to make fuller use of the stock, is part of the information dissemination process or forms part of the library's cultural and educational role.

The best format
In the next chapter we shall look at the technical side of the many methods of reproduction available to the librarian. The factors that will affect the decision can be summarized as follows:

1   *Volume of copies to be produced*
   (a) Very small: use photocopier, particularly if the copy consists chiefly of copies of pre-printed matter, eg contents lists of journals.
   (b) Small — say up to 500: use a stencil and absorption duplicator. If available the small offset litho machines are equally cost-effective.
   (c) Very small but colour wanted: spirit duplication is the only cheap system, but copies are limited in number.
   (d) Medium to large runs — 1,000 plus: use in-house offset litho or outside traditional printing. Use the latter particularly if stitching or binding is required since the printer will usually have facilities for folding, cutting, and binding.

2   *Appearance*
   (a) Average quality, or cheap and cheerful, standard duplicating. Using an electric stencil cutter some quite good covers can be produced from Letraset originals. Line drawings are possible, but photographs are rarely successful on an electric cutter.
   (b) Good quality, using offset litho with originals made either by typing directly onto a master, or by producing the master on a photocopying machine. Using golf-ball or daisy-wheel typewriters a good range of typefaces can be used on the same page; different type sizes can also be used. A 'print' effect can be obtained by reducing the typewritten page by, say, 50 per cent on a photocopying reducing machine

before making the master. Covers and title pages can be very elaborate, and include logos, if a 'paste-up' original is made before the master is produced. Photographs, etc are possible but their quality is sometimes suspect.

(c) High quality. Professional printing is essential; often this is not as costly as you may think, and small local printers can be a very good 'buy' for leaflet production. Photographs, etc can be introduced more easily using this method.

3   *Speed of production*

(a) 'Yesterday'. Most library work falls under this heading. The fastest method is photocopying, followed by duplicating, then offset, then printing.

(b) 'Tomorrow'. A reasonable job can be done using any methods except printing.

(c) 'Next month'. Usually all methods will compete in this time scale.

4   *Cost*

This is so often volume dependent that no easy answer is possible. When many thousands of copies are required, in-house offset litho or outside printing may well be the best bet. For small volume, absorption duplicating is usually much cheaper than photocopying.

Preparing material

Regardless of the reprographical system used to produce the end product the ways in which the material is prepared are similar in each case.

1   *Collection of material*

The material may be in the form of a bibliography or in normal prose, but each will require a list of headings under which the information is to be provided. The chapter headings of a book are a good example. Once the material is collected these headings may well need to be modified either by adding or removing whole headings or by providing sub-headings. Often the material will be collected on cards or loose-leaf paper so that internal reorganization is quite an easy matter and re-writing is thereby cut down to a minimum.

2   *First draft*
This depends on circumstances. Some will produce a
manuscript draft and work on and polish that; others will
dictate their material and get a first typewritten draft to
work on. In either case plenty of space should be left
between lines (two to three on a typewriter) so that
changes and corrections can be made clearly and easily.
If possible colleagues should be asked to comment on
this draft.

3   *Second draft*
This is normally typewritten on one side of A4 paper, in
double-line spacing with wide margins to accommodate
corrections. At this stage the insertion of illustrations is
considered and suitable places in the text marked. Spelling
should be standardized throughout the text, and size of
headings shown. The pages should not be bound or
stapled together, as this makes insertions and corrections
difficult. Pages (or folios as they are often called) should
be numbered and any extra pages added later. These
should be numbered 2a, etc.

The final length of the publication can be judged and
printing methods discussed. The format of the final
product also has to be considered. A5 and A4 are popular
sizes in libraries because of their ease of production.
However, one does see A4 folded twice to give a 'pocket
leaflet'.

The cost of these operations has to be considered as
well.

4   *Final copy*
For printing it is usual to produce this on single-sided
A4, in double spacing. However, some less traditional
methods call for different techniques. By setting tabu-
lators on the typewriter three columns can be produced
for two-fold A4 either on a stencil or for offset litho.
Similarly, A5 leaflets can be produced. Great care is
needed to produce clean copy; this is essential if it is
going directly onto an offset master for here every
fingerprint *will* print! The stencil is perhaps the most
flexible (after plain paper), since correction fluid can be
used to remove errors. Even so these can often be seen as
unclear letters on the final print.

5   *Printing and proofs*
On in-house offset litho the final copy is the end of the
road; the copies are made from that master. In outside
printing (most of which is still offset litho!) other stages
usually take place. These are:

(a) galley or slip proofs. The printer will represent your
original in a typeface you have selected with appropriate headings, italics, etc. Sometimes actual 'type'
will be set but increasingly printers are using photo-
setting. Galleys are often just columns of print up to
two feet long. These are checked for accuracy, and
this is the last chance to make changes without great
cost.
(See British Standards Institution publication BS
5261, Part 2.)

(b) Page proofs. The galleys are made up into actual
pages with page numbers, headlines, etc. The positions
of illustrations are shown. These pages are nowadays
laid out on a broad, ready for negatives to be made
for printing.

6   *Binding*
Most library materials are 'saddle stitched', ie stapled
through the folded edge. Some libraries use 'perfect'
binding for booklets, but this tends to be expensive in
comparison.

Correcting proofs
The British Standards Institution has produced BS 5261
Parts 1 and 2 (1975 and 1976) and these are generally
regarded as the 'bible' for proof correction.
    Many local printers have a much smaller card giving basic
symbols that their staff are used to seeing and should be
asked for copies of these.

Further reading
BS 5261 Parts 1 and 2.
Writers and artists yearbook 1984. A and C Black.
Chambers, Harry T *Copying duplicating and microfilm.*
Business Books, 1970.
Jennett, Sean *The making of books.* London, Faber &
Faber, 1973.

Project work

1 Collect three different samples of library publications and comment on their method of production.
2 List the 10 symbols in BS 5261 that you think are likely to be the most used.
3 Practise using these symbols (and any others) on copy going to a printer.
4 Outline the headings of a library booklet you would like to produce, give reasons for the quantity of copies you suggest be made and select the appropriate printing method.

Chapter Twelve

Library/resource centre equipment

Office practice forms part of the day to day routine in all types of library, therefore office machinery will be included in a library's inventory. Of prime importance, of course, is the typewriter which will be used for correspondence, compilation of booklists and bulletins, typing of readers' tickets and a hundred and one other routine tasks. The electric typewriter ensures even pressure and so produces a more attractive appearance. Offset litho masters must be produced on an electric typewriter using a special litho ribbon with a high grease content. A golf-ball typewriter is very useful as a variety of typefaces can be used, thus giving a very professional look to home-produced reports and book-lists. Modern typewriters of this type are often fitted with an erasing tape which enables typing errors to be corrected by using a special back-spacing key, re-typing the incorrect letter to obliterate it and then typing the correct letter on top. Obviously this gives a much more satisfactory result than that achieved by the use of erasers or erasing fluid. Sophisticated typewriters are available such as the vari-typer, which produces a layout like a page of a book with straight margins at both sides of the text, and a tape-typewriter, which produces punched tape. Larger libraries may have word processors.

Other office equipment to be found in libraries may include:

Adding machines or calculators to cope with statistics related to petty cash, issues, membership, etc. Some machines have a visual display and others produce a paper print-out.

Addressing machines/addressographs are used in libraries which offer a regular postal service to their clientele. Each client's address is typed on a mini-stencil protected by a cardboard mount, and these are filed in sequence ready for use on the machine which acts like a mini-printer.

Franking machines are obtainable from the Post Office. Letters and parcels would be weighed by library staff and franked to show the correct amount in lieu of sticking on postage stamps. Franking machines offer the advantages of dispensing with the purchase and stocking of sheets of stamps of varying values, and of speeding up delivery, as franked items go straight to the sorting office instead of being processed through the Post Office.

Telephones are essential and are used to receive reference inquiries and telephone renewals as well as for outgoing calls by library staff.

Telex

This is a fairly recent development in the field of telecommunications, and is proving its worth in quite a number of libraries. The equipment consists of a teleprinter, which resembles a typewriter, and a dialling unit. Each telex machine is connected by direct line to an automatic telex exchange.

Each subscriber's installation is given a telex number and an individual identification signal known as the 'answerback code', both of which appear in the United Kingdom Telex Directory. The Telex Directory is arranged in two sections; the first has entries in subscriber order (like a telephone directory), the second is arranged in 'answerback' order.

A telex subscriber can contact any other telex subscriber in this country merely by dialling. When the call is connected, the distant machine automatically sends its own 'answerback code' for identification by the caller as a check that he is through to the required number. The sender then types the message on the telex keyboard and the typed message appears in 'black and white' on a roll of paper on both the sender's machine and the receiver's machine.

Subscribers in the UK can communicate at any time of day or night, even when the receiving library is closed and the machine unattended. The receiving machine automatically identifies itself, and then records the message on the telex roll to be read and dealt with later.

Advantages of telex in libraries
1 Speed of communication. It is much quicker than the postal service and is excellent for inter-library loan requests.
2 Flexible timing. There is no need for a human recipient at the time of communication as the message is recorded and stored. It is useful where one library's hours differ from another's.

Disadvantages
1 Possibility of breakdown of machine or failure due to power cut.
2 Slips of telex paper can be easily lost or defaced. Requests, if not dealt with speedily, may be forgotten if no other record is kept. Telex operators usually have to spend a lot of time 'chasing' requests.
3 Open to error. The operator may make more mistakes when using a keyboard than when writing by hand.
4 Cost. There is a connection charge and an annual rental plus a charge for each call at rates which vary according to the distance between centres. In order to cut costs, some libraries have machines with the facility of pre-producing messages on perforated tape. This tape can then be fed into the machine when the telex connection is made to ensure that the message is transmitted at the maximum speed.

Television monitors and microcomputers
In this age of instant information retrieval, library users expect to find television sets with teletext facilities in their local libraries. Information 'pages' provided by the four TV channels are free and are accessed by keying in the required page number on a hand-held remote control device.

Some libraries also provide a Prestel/Micronet service. Nowadays, the television monitor is coupled to a keyboard, a microcomputer, and a telephone dialling unit. The user library has a password which is keyed in to facilitate identification and payment of expenditure incurred in using the Prestel/Micronet system. Prior to logging-off, a statement of expense incurred appears on the screen. The amount covers telephone charges as well as the cost of certain pages of information or programmes.

Many Prestel/Micronet information packages can be recorded on to a blank floppy disc inserted into the microcomputer and, again, the charge for this facility appears on the screen. Alternatively, numerous commercially produced programmes on floppy disc are available for purchase and the microcomputer and monitor can be used for playback of these programmes.

Large library systems may own a large computer and use it for ordering and cataloguing stock as well as basing the issue system on it. Smaller libraries may co-operate in a network and have shared access to a commercially-owned computer or may buy time on a computer belonging to another organization.

Reprographic equipment

Reprographic equipment of one kind or another is to be found in practically every library. The most common item of equipment is the coin-in-the-slot photocopier which is provided for public use. The term 'photocopier' is now loosely used as some of these copiers do not work on photographic principles.

Electrostatic copying machines

The electrostatic process, sometimes known as xerography, was invented in the USA in 1938. Machines are available for purchase or rental from manufacturers and a fee paid for each copy produced. The rental charge includes a maintenance agreement and engineers come at very short notice to repair faults.

On balance most libraries prefer to own their equipment than rent it.

The type of copier required by most libraries is a simple, basic machine which will produce a single-sided copy from an original book, periodical or document. Large and complex machines are available which will automatically produce double-sided copies and will collate multiple copies of successive pages. Some machines also have a reduction facility, eg from A3 to A4, A4 to A5. However, the majority of libraries would not make use of such complex features and prefer the small, table-top models which will do a basic job satisfactorily.

Method

The original, which may be an opened book, periodical, document or illustration, is placed face downwards on the glass platen of the machine. A rubber blanket is then brought over the top of the original to cut out extraneous light. Some machines have an indicator to align with the lower edge of the original so that the copy produced will be the required length.

When the power is switched on, the money inserted if it is a coin-in-the-slot machine, and the 'print-button' pressed, a light source within the machine shines on to the original. The image is then reflected via a series of mirrors on to an electrically charged, rotating selenium drum. The charge on the drum is discharged over those areas which correspond with the white or background areas of the original but the charge remains on those areas corresponding with the black text or illustrations. What remains on the selenium drum is therefore an inverted, invisible latent image.

Next a carbon powder or toner is shaken over the selenium drum. The powder adheres to the parts of the drum where the electrical charge remains but does not stick to the drum where the charge has been dispersed. The inverted image now appears in visible form on the drum.

A sheet of copy paper is drawn into the machine from the feed tray and the paper is electrically charged before it comes into contact with the selenium drum. The carbon powder transfers from the drum to the paper because it is drawn by an opposite electrical charge. At this stage the powder is just 'sitting' on the paper and would be easily smudged, so before the copy appears in the take-up tray the image is fixed by exposure to heat. The selenium drum is automatically cleaned by rotating in contact with a brush so loose particles of powder are removed in readiness for the next copy to be made.

As described, the process appears to be lengthy but it is really very rapid and the copy is produced in a few seconds. As stated earlier, the main purpose of electrostatic copiers is to produce single copies, but they will produce multiple copies very rapidly. Most machines are fitted with a pre-select button so that one can set the required number. The machine will stop automatically when the correct number of copies have been ejected. However, if multiple copies are required, other types of reprographic equipment may be preferable because of their economy.

Advantages of electrostatic copying

1   Simplicity of operation. The process is a direct one from original to copy without the production of any intermediate master.
2   Speed of production of copies.
3   Copies are of a high quality with dense black on white. In fact the intensity of the image can be adjusted so that the copy is sometimes better than the original.
4   Run-off paper is not expensive.
5   Copies do not fade, even when kept for a considerable period.

Disadvantages

1   The image on the copy is always black even when a coloured original is used. To achieve the effect of colour one has to feed coloured paper into the machine.
2   Difficulty may be experienced when coloured originals are copied in that certain colours, notably blue, do not copy well.
3   If the machine is in constant use the selenium drum may not be cleaned sufficiently and stray particles of carbon will appear as minute black spots on the copies. As this problem worsens, the copies tend to have a dirty appearance.
4   Paper sometimes becomes jammed in the machine, and great care must be taken in removing it otherwise the selenium drum may be damaged.
5   Rented machines are expensive in the long-term.

Spirit duplicating machines

Spirit duplication is probably the cheapest and easiest of the available reprographic methods. The quality of the copies produced, however, does not compare favourably with some other methods, notably offset lithography. Nevertheless, a spirit duplicator could be very useful in a children's library for the production of project worksheets or quiz forms.

Sometimes the process is referred to by the name of Banda but this is really a trade name for one make of spirit duplicator, Fordigraph being another. The method is as follows:

Materials and equipment

One can purchase blank paper masters from commercial suppliers. The master has a glossy side coated with kaolin and an uncoated reverse side. It is also necessary to have a supply of 'carbons'. These have no carbon content but resemble typewriter carbons, hence the loose usage of the term. Actually, they are sheets of paper coated with aniline dye which is commonly dark blue or purple, although rainbow packs are obtainable which include red, blue, green, yellow, brown and black. There is also a choice of long-run or short-run 'carbons' to match the number of copies to be produced. A short-run 'carbon' is suitable for up to 100 copies and a long-run 'carbon' will produce about 300 copies. In addition, a supply of coated, non-absorbent run-off paper is required on which the copies will be produced. Lastly, one needs a spirit duplicating machine and a supply of spirit solvent with which to top up the solvent container incorporated in the machine.

Preparation of a master

To prepare a master manually, a master sheet must be placed on top of a 'carbon' so that the glossy side of the master and the dye-coated side of the 'carbon' are in contact. Using a pencil or ballpoint pen the text/diagram is written, printed or drawn on the uncoated upper surface of the master, using firm pressure on a hard smooth surface. This transfers the dye from the 'carbon' to the coated side of the master, leaving a reverse image of what appears on the upper surface. Coloured work is achieved by using different colours of carbon for various parts of the image.

The master may also be produced by using a typewriter but a backing sheet should be used. The typescript will be fuzzy and indistinct without the smooth, firm surface which the backing sheet offers.

A further method of producing a master is to use a thermal (heat) copier. To do this the original image or typescript must be on a single sheet of paper and it must have carbon content. A special hectofilm unit is required. This is just a dye sheet attached to a master sheet to make a combined unit especially designed for use with a thermal copier. The 'original' must be placed image-upwards in a 'carrier' and the hectofilm unit placed on top of the original. The hectofilm unit will probably have a tissue interleaf and this should be removed. The carrier containing both items is then fed into the rotating rollers of the thermal copier and as it proceeds through the machine it activates an infra-red light. The heat produced causes the transfer of dye to the master at those areas which correspond with the carbon image on the original. Masters produced on a thermal copier are of one colour throughout and not multi-colour. Nowadays one can purchase pre-prepared masters and sometimes these are incorporated into educational books.

Production of copies

The spirit duplicating machine is prepared for use by placing a stack of run-off paper in the feed tray. It is wise to fan the paper to separate the sheets and let air in between them, otherwise several sheets might stick together and clog up the machine. The fluid-control button should then be moved to the 'on' position and the priming button pressed several times. This causes spirit fluid to moisten the felt pad in the duplicator. The prepared master is clamped around the metal drum so that the dye image is outermost. Then the drum is rotated manually, or automatically if an electrically-operated duplicator is used. At each rotation, one sheet of copy paper is fed into the machine where it is dampened with the spirit solvent. The moistened paper then comes into contact with the master and the spirit solvent causes the transfer of one layer of dye from the master to the copy paper. The copy is then ejected into a take-up tray where it quickly dries. As more and more copies are produced, so the amount of dye on the master is reduced layer by layer until the image on the copy paper becomes quite faint. To compensate for the decreasing amount of dye one can adjust the pressure control knob and press the copy paper more firmly to the master.

Advantages of spirit duplication

1   The equipment is cheap compared with that for other methods and the materials are comparable in cost.
2   The preparation of masters is simple and speedy.
3   Multi-coloured copies are easy to produce and there is no problem with 'register'.
4   Errors on the master can be erased by gently removing the layer of dye with a razor blade.

5   No skill is required in operating the machine.
6   Machines are robust and need very little maintenance.

Disadvantages
1   Copies are not of high quality. The text may appear slightly fuzzy, especially if the characters are as small as those produced by typewriter.
2   The number of copies that can be produced is limited.
3   Copies tend to fade, especially if left exposed to daylight, and some of the colours are not strong to begin with.
4   The operator needs to exercise care in handling materials to prevent dye from colouring the fingers.

Absorption duplicating machines
Absorption duplication is probably better known by trade names such as Roneo and Gestetner or by the term stencil duplicating. One may occasionally hear it referred to as cyclostyling or mimeographing. It is a widely used method which produces good quality copies at very reasonable cost. The method involves the following:

Materials and equipment
A stencil is the basic requirement of this process and it can be of several types:
(a) A stencil designed for use with a typewriter. This consists of a thin sheet of paper, similar to tissue paper but coated with wax, which is attached to a thicker paper backing sheet, and with a sheet of carbon as an interleaf between the two.
(b) A thermic stencil which is similar in appearance to the ordinary stencil but has a thinner wax sheet. There is no carbon interleaf but instead a sheet of tissue is attached to the unit so that it completely covers the upper surface of the waxed sheet. Thermic stencils are specially designed for use with a thermal copier.
(c) A paper-based or plastic stencil designed for 'cutting' on an electronic stencil cutter. On the latter a wax coating covers a thin sheet of plastic which is attached to a paper backing sheet. Plastic stencils are especially good for reproducing half-tone illustrations.
    The run-off paper must be thick and absorbent to cope with the thick layer of ink deposited on it by the duplicator.

The duplicating machine and a supply of ink are the final requirements.

Preparation of a master
To enable ink to penetrate the wax sheet and thus come into contact with the copy paper, the wax coating must be removed in areas corresponding to the required text or diagram. One can do this manually by using a stylus or a cutting tool designed for that purpose, but the most common method is to use a typewriter. The ribbon must be disengaged so that the metal typefaces strike the wax sheet directly. This ensures that the wax is cleanly cut and the characters are sharp. Problems can arise if an inexperienced typist strikes the keys too strongly as enclosed letters such as 'o' tend to drop out. Also, continued contact with the waxy surface may clog up the typefaces. To prevent these problems arising, some stencils are covered by a thin transparent plastic top sheet which meets the typefaces as they are struck yet does not prevent the cutting of the wax surface beneath. A carbon interleaf allows one to see what has been typed.

If a thermal copier is to be used in the preparation of the master, a special thermic stencil must be employed and the original text or diagram must be pre-prepared on a single sheet. The image must also have carbon content in order to activate the thermal copier. The original is placed face upwards on the stencil's backing sheet, the wax sheet is then placed over it and the tissue sheet on top of that. The thermic stencil is then fed through the rollers of the thermal copier where it activates an infra-red lamp. The heat melts the wax on those areas which correspond with the image areas of the original, and the melted wax is absorbed into the tissue sheet.

An electric stencil cutting machine has twin cylinders which rotate together on the same plane. The original, which must be a single sheet or text and/or illustrations, is clamped around the left hand cylinder and a special stencil fastened around the other cylinder. As both drums rotate a photo-electric scanning device travels line by line over the surface of the original detecting light and dark areas. Wherever the scanner 'reads' an image area it activates a stylus which correspondingly travels line by line across the stencil. The stylus emits tiny sparks which cut minute holes in the surface of the stencil.

Production of copies

If the stencil has a carbon interleaf it must be removed. The top edge of the stencil is then attached to the cylinder of the duplicating machine using the slots or perforations provided. The waxed sheet must be in contact with the cylinder. While the stencil is held taut, the cylinder is slowly rotated until the bottom edge of the wax sheet can be clamped in position. Wrinkling or creasing of the wax sheet must be avoided. The ink supply will have been checked and the cylinder rotated manually a few times while the inking lever is depressed. This ensures an even ink flow. The paper backing sheet can then be removed (leaving only the wax sheet around the cylinder). A supply of copy paper should be fanned out and stacked in the feed tray and this must be raised to the correct level for feeding into the machine. One or two copies may be produced manually to see whether the image is properly aligned and the margins are correct. The machine can then be switched to automatic and it will produce the number of copies stipulated by the pre-set counter. With each rotation of the cylinder, ink is forced through the holes in the waxed stencil and this ink is deposited on the copy paper as it is fed into the machine.

One stencil will normally produce up to 5,000 copies though it is claimed that 7,500 copies may be obtained from a good quality stencil. If a stencil is carefully removed from the cylinder after use and blotted to remove excess ink, it can be stored and re-used.

Advantages of absorption duplication
1   Equipment and materials are cheap.
2   Stencils are easily prepared by a variety of methods.
3   Errors on the stencil are easily rectified by coating with correction fluid and then writing or typing on top.
4   Duplicating machines are easy to operate.
5   A considerable number of copies can be produced from one stencil.
6   A good black and white image is achieved and there is no fading even when copies are stored for a lengthy period.
7   Stencils are re-usable.

Disdavantages
1   The layer of ink deposited is thick and this necessitates the use of absorbent copy paper with a rough texture.

2 Multi-colour work is difficult. The cylinder must be thoroughly cleaned before another colour of ink is used or the whole cylinder must be lifted out and replaced by another.
3 The operator may get ink on his/her hands and clothing.

Offset litho machines
The basic principle of offset lithography is that grease and water are mutually repellant.

Historical background
Legend has it that the principle underlying lithography was discovered quite by chance by a Bavarian printer named Senefelder (c.1796). One day he was sitting on a large stone on a Bavarian hillside eating his picnic lunch when it began to rain heavily. He stood up and began to collect his belongings when he noticed something odd about the stone he had been sitting on. Although the rain was falling on the stone it was not completely wet but showed a pattern of parallel lines where the rain water was not being absorbed by the porous stone. He realized that the lines corresponded to the ridges of his greasy corduroy trousers. Some grease had been transferred to the surface of the stone and the grease was repelling the rain water. Senefelder pondered over this fact as he walked back to the printing shop and decided that the principle could be put to use in printing.

Lithography as a printing process dates from the 19th century. Porous Bavarian limestone was used as this absorbs grease and water equally. The stone was first levelled to give a perfectly flat surface, then grained to give either a fine or coarse grain. The artist then drew, sketched or painted on the grained surface using greasy crayon, pen, brush, or even a finger. Normally black crayon or ink was used so that the artist could see what he was doing, but otherwise the colour was of no importance. As the surface would pick up any grease, the artist had to be careful not to leave unwanted fingerprints or greasy marks on the stone as they would show up in printing. However, chemicals could be used to remove unwanted grease or to 'fix' the required greasy drawing.

On completion of the drawing, the stone was placed in a flat-bed printing machine where it was wetted by damping rollers. The water was absorbed by the non-image background areas but rejected by the greasy areas. The stone was then 'inked-up' by the inking rollers and this time the greasy ink adhered to the greasy image but was repelled by the dampened background areas. The impression cylinder then pressed paper against the stone and the image was transferred to the paper.

In later years zinc or aluminium plates were used instead of stone as these were cheaper, less heavy and easier to store. The metal plates were grained to give a roughened surface which would hold ink or water.

Offset lithography

With offset lithography, there is no direct contact between the plate and the copy paper. Instead the image is first transferred to an intermediate surface, ie the blanket roller, and it is this which comes into contact with the copy paper. The image is the right way round on the master, reversed on the blanket cylinder and the right way round once more on the copy paper. The first offset litho machine (1875) was a flat-bed machine in which the image was transferred from card to metal and then to paper. Rotary machines are now used in which the image is transferred from a master or plate to a rubber blanket stretched tightly around the blanket cylinder and then to the copy paper.

Making a master or plate

1 *Direct image masters.* Paper masters are available on which the image can be produced manually using a special pen containing greasy ink or by typewriter using a special offset ribbon which has a high grease content. The image should be on the surface of the plate so it is important to use an electric typewriter which gives even pressure. Typing errors cannot be obliterated with a normal erasing fluid as this would print and appear as a blotch on the copies. Special erasers are available which gently remove the greasy letters ready for re-typing. Care must be taken not to get greasy fingerprints on the master.

2 *Paper plates produced by an electrostatic plate-maker.* The original, which may be a single typed or manually produced sheet, a montage, or a book or periodical is

placed face downwards on the glass platen of the electro-static copier. A rubber blanket or hinged lid covers the original to cut out extraneous light and then, at the push of a button, paper is fed into the machine and charged with electricity. A light then scans the original and the light is bounced back on to the charged paper. Light is reflected from the white or background areas of the original and the action of the light on the paper dissipates the electrical charge. No light is reflected from the black or image areas so the charge remains in the paper in areas corresponding to the image. When a coloured original is used, the machine can 'read' the colours only as different intensities of black or white. Thus some colours, particularly blue, do not reproduce well. As the paper progresses through the machine, toner or carbon powder is shaken onto it. The toner particles adhere to the electrically charged areas of the paper, thus forming a visible image. This image is then fixed by the action of a chemical solution and dried by heat before it emerges as a plate ready for printing.

There are various qualities of paper plate for short (150 copies), medium (1000 copies) or long (3000 copies) runs.

3 *Metal plates produced by a photographic process.* Sensitized aluminium plates produced photographically or on a plate-making machine utilizing ultra-violet light give the longest runs (25,000 to 40,000 copies) and the best quality copies. Professional printers use only metal plates. These plates can be stored and used again time after time provided they are wiped over with a gum solution after each use to prevent oxydization.

4 *Polyester plates.* These are a fairly recent innovation and give good results. Up to 5,000 copies can be produced from a polyester plate. Plates can be stored and re-used.

5 *Litho scan plates produced on an electronic scanner.* With this method, the original text, illustration or montage must be on a flat sheet of paper. This is clamped around the left-hand cylinder of the electronic scanner. A blank plate is then clamped around the right-hand cylinder.

When the machine is set in motion a scanning device travels backwards and forwards over the original as it rotates, and transmits an electronic signal whenever it 'reads' a black or image area. This signal activates a sparking device which cuts holes in the rotating plate to correspond with the image areas of the original.

Printing or duplicating on an offset litho machine
The paper, polyester or metal plate is clamped around the plate cylinder on the machine. Fountain solution (ie water with additives which make it less miscible with ink and slow down evaporation) is transferred from the fount tray via a series of fountain rollers until it comes into contact with the plate. The background areas of the plate are dampened by the fountain solution but the greasy image areas on the plate repel the fountain solution.

The plate then comes into contact with the ink which has been carried by a series of inking rollers from the ink-tray. This time, ink adheres to the greasy image areas on the plate, but is repelled by the wet non-image areas.

The plate cylinder is then brought into contact with the blanket cylinder where the ink image is transferred to the rubber blanket. The image is in reverse as it appears on the blanket roller.

Paper is then fed into the machine from the feed trays and the paper is pressed against the blanket roller by the impression cylinder. The image is thus transferred to the paper and appears the right way round. There is a pre-set counter to ensure the correct number of copies is produced.

Only a very thin layer of ink is transferred from the blanket to the paper. Consequently the machine will print on to very thin tracing paper (like fine greaseproof paper). However, it will also print on to three-sheet card or on to self-adhesive labels on backing sheets.

Cleaning the rubber blanket
Most offset litho machines now have the facility for cleaning the rubber blanket and rollers automatically. A bottle containing blanket wash solvent is incorporated in the machine and the process is activated by depressing and holding a lever.

Colour printing

A wide range of coloured inks is available for offset litho printing. The ink tray would be removed, the rollers and blanket cleaned automatically with blanket wash and a new ink tray containing the required colour of ink inserted. A separate plate is required for each colour. The first colour would be printed and then the paper fed back into the machine for printing with the second colour. Register is quite accurate on most offset litho machines so good quality four-colour work can be produced.

Advantages of offset litho

1   Copies are of excellent quality. The first copy is as good as the last, and all are as good as the original.
2   Illustrations and colour work can be of comparable quality to letterpress printing.
3   Direct masters are cheaper than most stencils and are as easy to prepare.
4   Indirect masters are very quickly and easily made and are quite cheap.
5   Many qualities of paper can be used including thin, cheap paper.
6   The method uses very little ink, and copies are virtually dry on delivery.
7   Copies are long-lasting and do not fade.
8   Automatic machines ensure that the operator does not get ink on hands or clothing.

Disadvantages

1   The capital cost of equipment is high (about £3,000 for a complete system of offset litho duplicating machine and plate-maker/fixer.).
2   Skill is required in operating the machine.

Thermal copying machines

Thermal copiers have already been mentioned in connection with the production of masters for use with other reprographic methods. The machines, though small, have many uses. These include:

1   Making one-off opaque copies from a single sheet original. The quality of reproduction is not high and appears

greyish rather than true black on white. Copies are liable to fade if left exposed to sunlight.

2   Making overhead projection transparencies. These are quickly and easily made and provided one has a good original the OHPs are of high quality.
3   Making masters for spirit duplication.
4   Making thermic stencils for absorption duplication.

Method

The original must be a single sheet — it will not copy directly from a periodical or book — and the image must have carbon content. The original is placed in contact with the copy paper, acetate sheet, hectofilm unit or thermic stencil, and in most cases the two are put into a carrier. The carrier is merely a cardboard backing sheet with a gauze or plastic top sheet and its purpose is to assist the copy to travel through the rollers of the machine. The electric power is switched on, the dial set to control the speed of travel and then the carrier is fed into a slot in the machine and taken up by rollers. This activates an infra-red lamp inside the machine and the heat from the lamp is intensified by the carbon areas of the original. This intensified heat is radiated back to the copy paper where the sensitized coating is 'scorched' in those areas corresponding to the image areas of the original.

Thermography is a simple method which is of most value when only one copy or master is required. It would not be used for the production of multiple copies as the machine must be fed manually before each copy is produced.

Dual spectrum machines

These machines, though quite small in size, incorporate two processes in one. At the top of the machine is a glass platen on which the original is placed in contact with a light-sensitive intermediate sheet. The original may be a single sheet, a periodical or a book. The lid of the machine is adjustable so that it can cope with varying thicknesses of original. The purpose of the lid is to prevent extraneous light affecting the light-sensitive paper. A timing control is set prior to pressing a push-button which activates a light source within the machine so that the correct exposure can be given. When the lamp switches itself off, the intermediate sheet can be separated from the original. At this stage there is only a latent image on the intermediate, ie the light sensitive coating has been affected by exposure to light, and an image corresponding to the image on the original is present but is invisible to the naked eye.

The next stage of the process involves the feeding of the intermediate sheet, which is in contact with a sheet of copy paper, through the lower part of the machine which is really a thermal copier. The action of the infra-red lamp causes the transfer of the latent image to the copy paper.

In some ways, the dual spectrum machine overcomes some of the drawbacks of the ordinary thermal copier in that it can cope with a greater variety of originals and these can be in coloured non-carbon inks. On the other hand, it is a two stage process and therefore is more time-consuming and more expensive.

Dyeline copying machines
Dyeline or diazo machines are seldom used in libraries. Their main purpose is to produce copies of large plans or maps such as would be needed in an architect's office or town planning department.

Method
The original, known as a translucency, is normally a line drawing on a sheet of translucent paper which resembles tracing paper or greaseproof paper. A thin sheet of polyester film may also be used. A sheet of sensitized paper of identical size is then required. This paper is coated with diazonium salts.

The original is placed on top of the sensitized copy paper so that both are facing upwards and the two are fed together into the machine. Inside the machine is a rotating pyrex lamp which emits ultra-violet light. The light is reflected from the non-image areas of the original, causing the chemicals in the sensitized copy paper to become inert. Where no light is reflected, ie in areas corresponding to the image on the translucency, the chemical coating remains, leaving a latent image on the copy paper. In order to render the image visible, the copy paper must be developed.

Machines differ in the developing process. The most common method is to expose the copy paper by passing it through a trough of developing fluid. The other methods utilize ammonia gas, heat or pressure. If ammonia gas is used, care must be taken to duct the gas through an external ventilator to prevent the operator being overcome by fumes. Ammonia-developed copy paper is capable of producing images in black, blue, sepia or reddish-brown.

Advantages of dyeline copying
1   Machines are uncomplicated and easy to operate.
2   Materials are relatively inexpensive.
3   Machines can cope with very large originals/copies.

Disadvantages
1   The original must be translucent.
2   Materials have a short shelf life, as the sensitized coating deteriorates with time.
3   Copies are the same size as the original. There is no facility for reduction/enlargement.
4   Copies fade, especially if left exposed to sunlight.
5   The ammonia method of developing poses problems of smell and fumes.

Copyright and libraries
Libraries lend many types of copyright works including books, music, artistic works, gramophone records and cassettes. Some libraries also lend films and videotapes. However the loan of these materials by libraries is in no way restricted by copyright law and there is no need to seek the permission of the copyright owner. The Copyright Act includes a definition of the term 'library' but it is a very wide definition which really includes all types of library except commercial lending libraries which presumably have indirect profit-making motives.

    Besides the lending of materials, most libraries offer a photocopying service and in this connection definite rules must be complied with. For a library to provide a copy of a periodical article without infringing copyright laws,
1   the library must be non-profit-making;
2   the person requesting the copy must satisfy the librarian that he requires it for research or private study;
3   Only *one* copy of the article may be produced for any one person;
4   only one article in a publication may be copied;

5   the person supplied with the article must pay the library a sum which covers the cost of its production;
6   a form of declaration should be completed and signed by the person requesting the copy.

The form is normally set out as follows:

```
                    COPYRIGHT ACT
           FORM OF DECLARATION AND UNDERTAKING
                (Statutory Instrument 1957 no.868)

    To.  The librarian

    PLEASE USE BLOCK CAPITALS

    1)   I, (name)..........
         of (firm)..........
         (address)..........
                  ..........
         (postal code)......              Telephone......
         hereby request you to make and supply to me a copy of
         the following periodical article which I require for the
         purpose of research or private study.

         NAME OF PERIODICAL..........
         VOLUME/ISSUE NUMBER ... DATE ... PAGES ...
         AUTHOR OF ARTICLE..........
         TITLE OF ARTICLE...........

    2)   I have not previously been supplied with a copy of the
         above-named article by any librarian.

    3)   I undertake that if a copy is supplied to me, I will not
         use it except for the purposes of research or private
         study.

                    Signature..............
                    Date      ..............
```

Similar restrictions apply to copying parts of books, plays and musical scores but in addition:
1   the part copied must not be a substantial part of the original;
2   if the name and address of the copyright owner is known to the librarian, he must seek that person's permission to make the copy.

Microform copies of entire works may not be made without the permission of the copyright owner, and the copying of gramophone records is not permitted at all.

Public Lending Right

The Public Lending Right Act was passed in Great Britain in 1979 and two Statutory Instruments relating to the PLR scheme appeared in May 1982 (no 719) and March 1983 (no 480). The Act of Parliament was passed in response to a demand by authors that they should receive payment from libraries for the loan to the public of books which those authors have written. This is on the grounds that sales of their books would increase and therefore the authors would receive a larger sum in royalties if members of the public were not able to borrow books free of charge from the public library. The 1979 Act recognized the author's right to payment but the details of how the money was to be levied and paid to authors were not fixed until Statutory Instrument 480 received Parliamentary Approval in 1982.

The scheme operates in the following way — the author must complete a separate application for each book he has written in order to register himself and the book in the PLR scheme. If a second or subsequent edition is published a new registration form must be submitted. Payment will not be made to authors who are not registered. Joint authors up to a maximum of two must also register on the same application form as the main or first-named author. Indeed payment will not be made to any of the co-authors unless all are registered. If one of the co-authors dies before registering in the PLR scheme the other(s) cannot register either and therefore have to forego payment. An illustrator of a book is deemed to be a 'co-author' and is therefore eligible for registration but editors, compilers and translators are not eligible. Co-authors have to agree the proportion of payment which each is to receive and this is stated on the registration form. Authors must register in their own name and not a pseudonym or maiden name under which the book may be written.

Payment of the author is based on the number of times his book is borrowed and purchased by libraries. This raises the anomaly of reference books or books put into the lending stocks of some libraries and the reference collections of others. A further anomaly is that payment is based on loans from public libraries. Loans from university, college, school, industrial and other special libraries are not considered. Furthermore to be eligible for the PLR scheme a book must have a minimum of 32 pages or 24 pages if it is mainly poetry or drama.

The method chosen for determining the number of loans is as follows. Sixteen public libraries are selected as a sample and these libraries send a monthly issue record to the PLR

office. Ten of the sixteen libraries selected have book issues
of more than 500,000 per year, the remaining six have fewer
than 500,000. The record is in the form of a magnetic tape
or cassette therefore the libraries chosen will be those operating a computer-based issuing system such as datapen. The
PLR office extracts the information about loans of registered
books from these tapes so the participating libraries are
involved in very little extra work. The PLR computer compares the file of registered authors/registered editions of their
works with the file of loans computed from the sixteen
libraries. The use of ISBNs makes this task easier but where
a book has no ISBN some other identification such as a BNB
or LASER 'ff' number is used.

The resultant figure is grossed up so that payment can be
calculated. There is a fixed minimum payment and a fixed
maximum payment and these monies are taken from a
central PLR fund. Payments to authors commenced in the
spring of 1984.

Practical assignments
1   Make a master and produce a few copies using
    (a) a spirit duplicator, or
    (b) an absorption duplicator (Roneo, Gestetner).
2   Consult the Telex Directory to discover the answerback
    code of the library in which you work or of which you
    are a member.
3   If there are libraries in your locality which offer Teletext
    and Prestel/Micronet, make a comparison of the range of
    information available in each.

Written assignments
1   Describe the method and outline the advantages and
    disadvantages of one of the following reprographic
    processes:
    (a) offset lithography
    (b) electrostatic copying
    (c) absorption duplication
    (d) spirit duplication
2   What is the application to libraries of
    (a) Copyright law *and*
    (b) Public Lending Right.

Bibliography

Brophy, Brigid *A guide to Public Lending Right.* Gower, 1983.

Flint, Michael F *A user's guide to copyright.* Butterworth, 1979.

New, Peter G *Reprography for librarians.* London. Clive Bingley, 1975.

Copyright law as it relates to specific materials

I. Type of work subject matter	Governing section of Act	II. Term of copyright	III. Restricted acts	IV. General exceptions	V. First owner
1. *Literary* (Books, newspapers, magazines, catalogues, letters, etc.) *Dramatic* (Plays, operas, screenplays, mimes, pantomimes, choreographic works, etc.) *Musical* (Classical and popular music and songs (*not* including sound recordings))	2	A. Life of author plus 50 years; or B. If not published, performed, sold or broadcast in author's lifetime; then 50 years from end of calendar year when first so done.	A. Reproducing the work in any material form. B. Publishing the work. C. Performing the works in public D. Broadcasting the work. E. Causing the work to be transmitted to subscribers to a diffusion service. F. Making an adaptation. G. Doing, in relation to an adaptation, any of A. to E.	A. Fair dealing: (i) for research or private study; (ii) for criticism or review with an acknowledgement; (iii) for reporting current events: (a) in a newspaper magazine or similar periodical with an acknowledgement; (b) by broadcasting or film. B. Reproducing for judicial proceedings or reports thereof. C. Reading or recitation in public (not broadcast) by one person of a reasonable extract, with an acknowledgement. D. Including a short passage in schools' collections (see chapter 18). E. Broadcast 'ephemeral right' (see chapter 24). F. Recording a musical work under the compulsory licence provisions (see chapter 20).	A. Author; or B. If made in course of employment under a contract of service with newspaper, magazine, periodical when employer will be first owner of newspaper, magazine etc. rights and author will be first owner of copyright for all other media; or C. If made in course of employment under contract of service (other than newspaper, etc.: employer will own

I Type of work/ subject matter	Governing section	II Term of copyright of Act	III Restricted acts	IV. General exceptions	V. First owner
6 *Sound recordings*	12	As 3	A. Making a record embodying in the recording B. Causing the recording to be heard in public. C. Broadcasting the recording.	A. Records previously published in UK by licence of owner but not bearing date of first recording. B. Causing recordings to be heard in public: (i) at premises where people reside as part of amenities of premises; (ii) as part of charitable of similar non-profit making body provided no charge is made. C. Compulsory licence provisions (see chapter 20).	A. The maker-being the person who owns the record when the recording is made; or B. The person who commissions the making of the sound recording and pays or agrees to pay for it in money or money's worth.
8 *Television broadcasts*	14	50 years from end of calendar year in which broadcast was made.	A. Making, otherwise than for private purposes, a cinematograph film or copy of such film. B. Making, otherwise than private purposes, a sound recording or a record embodying such recording. C. Causing it to be seen or heard in public by a paying audience. D. Re-broadcasting it.	A. As 1 B. above. B. People who are residents or inmates of premises are not a paying audience. C. Members of club where television viewing facilities are incidental to main purposes of club and not to a paying audience.	The BBC or the IBA, as the case may be

9 *Sound broadcasts*	14								
10 *Published editions of works*	15	As8	25 years from end of calendar year in which edition was first published.	As8, except C.	The making by any photographic or similar process of a reproduction of the typographical arrangement of the edition.	As8.	The making by or on behalf of a librarian of a reproduction of a typographical arrangement of the edition (see chapter 17).	As8.	The publisher of the edition

Note: *Government publications*:

(a) Term is 50 years from date of publication.

(b) Crown is owner of all works or subject matters (except TV and sound broadcasts) made by or under the direction and control of the Government.

Index